BENSON and **HEDGES**.
SNOOKER YEAR

SEVENTH EDITION EDITED BY TERRY SMITH
ASSOCIATE EDITOR STEPHEN HENDRY

PELHAM BOOKS

PELHAM BOOKS

Published by the Penguin Group
27 Wrights Lane, London W8 5TZ, England
Viking Penguin Inc., 40 West 23rd Street, New York, New York 10010, USA
Penguin Books Australia Ltd, Ringwood, Victoria, Australia
Penguin Books Canada Ltd, 2801 John Street, Markham, Ontario, Canada L3R 1B4
Penguin Books (NZ) Ltd, 182-190 Wairau Road, Auckland 10, New Zealand

Penguin Books Ltd, Registered Offices: Harmondsworth, Middlesex, England

First published by Pelham Books simultaneously in hardback and paperback 1990

Typeset, printed and bound in Great Britain by
BPCC Hazell Books Ltd
Member of BPCC Ltd
Aylesbury, Bucks, England

A CIP catalogue record for this book is available from the British Library

ISBN 0 7207 1955 0

CONTENTS

Acknowledgements 4

My Message to Steve Davis: I Aim to Stay at Number 1 5

Sponsor's Introduction 9

What's on Where in the 1990/91 Season 10

Who Said This? 11

Where the Players are Ranked and How They Pick up Points 14

The New Arrivals for 1990/91 18

Where Did All the Money Go? 22

The Top Thirty-two:
Best Performances and Who Won What Where and When 26

The Way They Were . . . But Who Are They? 62

Reflections on a Tournament Year 64

Who Said That? 102

Earthquakes on Thursday Island and Billiards in a Lions' Den! 104

Snooker's a Funny Game 110

The Man Behind the Mic: 'Whispering' Ted Lowe 112

How the Benson and Hedges Irish Masters Was Born 119

How Dripping Water Helped the Career of Referee John Williams 125

A Thai in Bradford: James Wattana 130

Allison Fisher: a Talented Young Woman in a Man's World 135

Snooker Snippets 141

The Changing Face of Billiards 142

The Amateur Scene 145

Rules of the Game of Snooker 151

Rules of the Game of English Billiards 156

ACKNOWLEDGEMENTS

The compilation of the *Benson and Hedges Snooker Year* is a demanding but enjoyable end-of-season race against time. Needless to say, there are many people who help ensure that it reaches the bookshops on time.

First, I must thank Stephen Hendry, world champion, world number 1, and the associate editor of the *Snooker Year*. Stephen takes a colourful look at his early career and then previews the season ahead when he is determined to stay at the top of the snooker tree.

Of course, my friends in the press room have again provided excellent articles. They are: Alexander Clyde (*Evening Standard*), Bob Holmes (*Evening Standard* and *Observer*), Bruce Beckett (Press Association) and Kevin Hughes.

The WPBSA and B&SCC and referees John Williams and John Street have helpd tremendously with the gathering of information, while Roger Lee, arguably the game's most informed historian, has taken a light-hearted journey down memory lane.

Photographs have played an important part in the *Snooker Year* over the years and additional material has been provided by Frank Fennell (on pages 12, 13, 39, 120, 122, 124, 128), Trevor Jones (on pages 5, 27, 30, 31, 33, 35, 36, 42, 47, 103, 134), John Hawken (on pages 11 (left), 15 (top), 49, 58, 114) and Colin McMorris (on page 38).

This is the fourth year that I have edited the *Snooker Year* and three female members of the 'team' have, despite my occasional show of petulance, stayed 'loyal'. They are: my wife Eileen, who checks all the important statistical material; Pat Mead, a veritable star on the word processor; and Ruth Baldwin, who has so conscientiously edited the copy. This seventh edition was designed by Sandie Boccacci who has produced such fine lay-outs.

Finally, my thanks yet again go to Benson and Hedges for allowing me to write the *Snooker Year* and to Roger Houghton and Pelham Books for once again publishing a book that is now firmly established on the snooker circuit.

MY MESSAGE TO STEVE DAVIS: I AIM TO STAY AT NUMBER 1

by Stephen Hendry

The 1989/90 season was the greatest of my life and I was thrilled to be invited as the Associate Editor of the *Benson and Hedges Snooker Year*. The Benson and Hedges Masters is one of the most prestigious tournaments on the circuit and I have been fortunate enough to win it for the past two seasons.

Shortly after I captured the Masters title in 1990 came the most unbelievable moment of my life as I stepped up to collect the Embassy World Championship trophy in front of a sell-out crowd at the Crucible Theatre in Sheffield. It was an occasion I will never forget and something I had dreamed of ever since I started playing nine years ago. I was overwhelmed by the atmosphere and didn't really appreciate what was going on until the after-match party when I was surrounded by my family and friends. Then I knew that it was all for real and that I had become the youngest world champion at twenty-one.

And what made it even more remarkable was the fact that I had been playing my great friend Jimmy White in the final, because Jimmy was the player I idolised as a young teenager trying to make the grade. I have always said that Steve Davis is the greatest player, but I love the way that Jimmy approaches the game, the speed of his potting and the sheer pleasure that he gives millions of people.

Of course, I would love to have beaten Davis in the final because he was the defending world champion, but the Whirlwind had already put paid to Steve's hopes when he beat him 16–14 in the semi-final.

My mum Irene and my dad Gordon

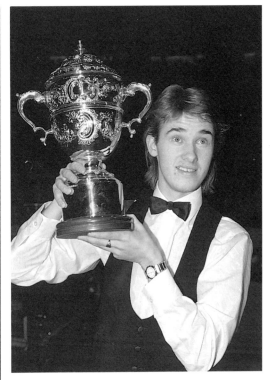

The Master again: Stephen Hendry after retaining the Benson and Hedges Masters title.

were there to witness this fantastic moment and, of course, so was my manager, Ian Doyle. Ian has guided my career since I turned professional in 1985, and although he has 'bullied' me on occasions I

Taking the reins: Stephen Hendry and Steve Davis, the world's top two players, after signing a £100,000 deal to compete in the Rothmans Centenary Challenge.

now know that all the hard work has been well worth it.

In the summer of 1988 I spent most of the time working on my golf handicap and stayed away from the practice table. Ian used to nag me to practise, but I reckoned that as British Open champion I could carry all before me the following season. It didn't quite work out that way, and in the 1988/89 season I didn't win a ranking tournament though I was fortunate to have become, at twenty, the youngest winner of the Benson and Hedges Masters. I sat down with Ian and discussed the future and I soon realised that the summer was not only for golf but also for working hard on my game in preparation for the 1989/90 season. As usual Ian was proved right and I started winning straight away, capturing six titles and also retaining the Benson and Hedges Masters. Then, of course, I took the World Championship as well, followed by the Continental Airlines London Masters. It was an incredible season for me.

I read with interest that Barry Hearn, who runs the rival Matchroom organisation, has declared 'war' on our Cuemasters team. That suits me just fine. There is nothing like a bit of good healthy competition to keep me on my toes. I also noticed that Mr Hearn said that Hadrian's Wall was built to keep out the Scots and that he didn't like me coming to England to 'pillage the trophies'. I just hope I can keep on pillaging for a good few years to come!

It's great to see that Steve Davis is going to play in all the ranking tournaments this season and that includes the overseas events as well. I was disappointed when he dropped out of three tournaments in Hong

Kong, Thailand and Dubai last season because he is always a tough man to beat and snooker needs him playing in *every* event. Now he's back in business for all tournaments, but I can tell him I am determined to keep hold of my number 1 position in the world rankings. Davis had been number 1 since 1983 and I am honoured to be in that position this season. Hearn said that Davis would now be like a 'wounded tiger', and if that's the case we should be in for a fantastic season in 1990/91.

What does the future hold? Snooker will certainly grow on a massive scale in years

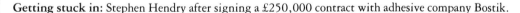

Getting stuck in: Stephen Hendry after signing a £250,000 contract with adhesive company Bostik.

to come and I think it was inevitable that the game would go completely open. From 1991/92 any player from anywhere in the world can enter professional tournaments. That has got to be good for the game and now we must spread the snooker message all over the globe.

Last season the top four players in the

Winning duo: Stephen Hendry and manager Ian Doyle plus the World Championship trophy.

world, Davis, John Parrott, White and myself, reached the semi-final stages of the World Championship. Now I think there are some good young players who could start challenging us at the top – star performers like Darren Morgan, Nigel Bond and Gary Wilkinson. But this is only the tip of the iceberg and I think the real talent of the game has yet to emerge. I

have seen so many good amateur players out there that when they eventually turn professional next season they will turn the game upside down.

A lot of people have asked me how I started playing snooker. I was about twelve when my mum and dad bought me a table for Christmas and almost immediately I started knocking in a few breaks. My dad realised I might have a talent for the game and in a matter of weeks I had knocked in breaks of 50 or 60. I suppose I was lucky that I scored my first century at the age thirteen, within a year of picking up a cue for the first time.

So where do I go this season? Of course, I would love to retain the titles I have already won, but I just want to remain as consistent as I was last season. I worked hard during the summer because I was world champion, but I decided not to do so many exhibitions, concentrating instead on the endorsements, advertising and sponsorship market. I aim to be very fresh for the start of this season because now I am world champion I am a marked man.

> ### WHO SAID THAT?
> 'Steve Davis is a legend and I will never write him off, but sadly his best days are gone.'
> ▲
> *– Ian Doyle, the manager of Stephen Hendry.*

Overall, snooker has a brilliant future. There are lots of great young players on the way up, the worldwide interest is gradually growing and the television viewing figures are holding up very well. Roll on the World Championship – I am looking for my second title.

SPONSOR'S INTRODUCTION

Welcome to the Seventh Edition of the *Benson and Hedges Snooker Year* which once again has been skilfully compiled by Editor Terry Smith to provide an invaluable reference source for snooker fans and an enjoyable and entertaining read for anyone with an interest in the game.

The start of a new snooker decade was hailed by the arrival of a new world champion in Stephen Hendry whom we are delighted to welcome as Associate Editor. Stephen commences the 1990/91 season as the official WPBSA world number 1 following a highly successful season in which he regained his Benson and Hedges Masters title at Wembley in the competition's sixteenth year.

Benson and Hedges continue to support snooker at the grassroots level and this season we add the Benson and Hedges Welsh Senior Championship to our existing sponsorship of the Benson and Hedges Snooker Challenge for Scottish amateurs. For the second year running, over 100 Scottish snooker clubs entered the Benson and Hedges Challenge, confirming the strength of the sport at a non-professional level and providing encouragement for future years.

WHAT'S ON WHERE IN THE 1990/91 SEASON

PROPOSED SNOOKER TOURNAMENT DATES

1990

Jun 3–12	Rothmans Grand Prix (prelims) 555 Asian Open (prelims) Dubai Duty Free Classic (prelims) StormSeal UK Open (prelims) European Open (prelims)	Norbreck Castle Hotel, Blackpool (0253 53488)
Sep 2–11	Mercantile Credit Classic (prelims) Pearl Assurance British Open (prelims) 555 Asian Open (to last 16) Dubai Duty Free Classic (to last 16) European Open (to last 16)	Norbreck Castle Hotel, Blackpool (0253 53488)
Sep 12–16	Regal Masters	Motherwell Civic Centre
Sep 26–28	International Tournament	Trentham Gardens, Stoke-on-Trent
Oct 8–21	Rothmans Grand Prix	Hexagon Theatre, Reading (0734 591591)
Oct 29–Nov 3	555 Asian Open	Guangchou, China
Nov 5–11	Dubai Duty Free Classic	Al Nasr Stadium, Dubai
Nov 16–Dec 2	StormSeal UK Open	Guild Hall, Preston (0772 58858)
Dec 6–15	World Matchplay	Brentwood Centre, Brentwood (0277 229621)
Dec*	Benson and Hedges Satellite	Masters Club, Glasgow

1991

Jan 1–12	Mercantile Credit Classic	Bournemouth International Centre
Feb 3–10	Benson and Hedges Masters	Wembley Conference Centre (081 900 1234)
Feb 17–Mar 2	Pearl Assurance British Open	Assembly Rooms, Derby (0332 255800)
Mar 9–17	European Open	Lyon, France (prov)
Mar 23–Apr 2	Embassy World Championship (prelims)	Guild Hall, Preston (0772 58858)
Apr 2–7	Benson and Hedges Irish Masters	Goffs, Co. Kildare, Republic of Ireland
Apr 20–May 6	Embassy World Championship	Crucible Theatre, Sheffield (0742 769922)

PROPOSED BILLIARDS TOURNAMENT DATES

1990

Oct 5–6	World Matchplay Championship	Moscow, USSR
Dec 16–22	World Championship	Brisbane, Australia

1991

Jan 25–26	British Open	Barbican Centre, London
Mar 28–Apr 3	Strachan UK Championship	Bolton Town Hall, Bolton
	Strachan UK One-cushion Championship	
	Strachan UK Under-16 and Under-19 Championships	
	Strachan Ladies Championship	
May 23–27	European Biathlon (Billiards/Carom)	Antwerp, Belgium

*Dates to be arranged.
All dates and venues are subject to change without prior notification.
Telephone numbers of venue box offices are given where applicable.

WHO SAID THIS?

'If you have a misted-up wristwatch, put it in a rice storage jar for three days and the moisture will clear.'

– a local telling one of the professional players how to clear his watch face during the humid weather at the Hong Kong Open.

'Good luck to Stephen, but it was inevitable that I would lose my number 1 spot. There was a time when I chased points like everyone else, but now the ranking points have become devalued.'

– Steve Davis after dropping out of the 555 Asian Open in Bangkok and hearing that Stephen Hendry had taken over his provisional number 1 place.

'Alain is a tough competitor and it was like chopping down a giant redwood.'

– Steve Davis after beating Alain Robidoux (below) 6–3 in the semi-final of the BCE International.

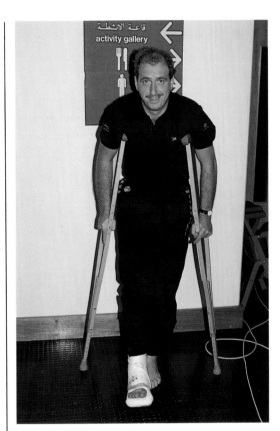

'I dragged off the reporter, put Alex Higgins in a chair and then fell down some stairs.'

– Midlands professional Jim Chambers (above) talking about an incident in a disco in Dubai that unfortunately ended with him in hospital with badly torn ligaments.

'I would like to announce my retirement from professional snooker. I don't want to be part of it. I would like to see Cecil Parkinson and Maggie Thatcher do a probe into snooker and then we would actually find out the real truth. This game is the most corrupt in the world.'

– Alex Higgins announcing his 'retirement' after a 10–5 first-round defeat by Steve James in the Embassy World Championship.

'It's the first time I have beaten Hallett in four attempts. If he had beaten me again, he could have put me on his mantelpiece.'

– *Stephen Hendry after his 6–1 win over Mike Hallett in the quarter-finals of the Regal Masters.*

'I am disgusted with Barry Hearn because I had a ridiculous itinerary. I was shattered. If Barry paid more attention to snooker, it would not have happened.'

– *Dennis Taylor after his 5–4 defeat by Willie Thorne in the first round of the Benson and Hedges Masters.*

'Dennis did have three matches in three days, but he was accompanied by a chauffeur. I don't consider that to be an arduous schedule.'

– *Barry Hearn replying to Dennis Taylor's comments.*

'Higgins said: "I come from Shankhill, you come from Coalisland and the next time you go back to Northern Ireland I will have you shot." '

– *Dennis Taylor after a disagreement behind the scenes with Alex Higgins at the British Car Rental World Cup final.*

'I was there when Alex Higgins threatened to have Dennis Taylor shot. There were some diabolical things said.'

– *John Spencer, chairman of the WPBSA, who witnessed the row between Dennis Taylor and Alex Higgins at the British Car Rental World Cup final.*

'I wish to apologise for the remarks made to Dennis Taylor, said in the heat of the moment.'

– *Alex Higgins the day after his row with Dennis Taylor at the British Car Rental World Cup final.*

'With Jimmy's ability it's nothing short of disgraceful that he hadn't won a tournament in the UK for nearly three years. He must be fed up with people talking about Davis and Hendry, but that's been his own fault because he has not been a winner. It's fitting he should be the player to win the last tournament of the 1980s and now the 1990s are down to him.

– *manager Barry Hearn speaking after Jimmy White had won the Everest World Matchplay.*

I have got my enthusiasm back and some of that's down to Stephen Hendry. I enjoy watching him and he is good for the game.'

– *Jimmy White (left) on his final victory in the Everest World Matchplay.*

'There is no way I will go out of the top sixteen – I will die to stay there. Money is a big incentive to me and if I could not stay in the top sixteen I would pack it all in and do coaching for a living.'

– *Terry Griffiths (above).*

'All the kids want to do today is smash up the pack and pot balls. There is a lot more to snooker than that.'

– *Terry Griffiths.*

'I went to the optician and received the most disappointing piece of good news I have ever had. My eyes were OK.'

– *Cliff Thorburn joking about his loss of form which he thought might have been caused by eyesight problems.*

'Ian Doyle convinced me I could be a winner, that I would win a major title. I owe Ian a great debt.'

– *Mike Hallett after beating Dene O'Kane 9–8 to win his first major title in the Hong Kong Open.*

'Mike does everything that a professional sportsman shouldn't do – going to night-clubs, wining and dining and playing golf when he should be practising. I have taken away all but one of his credit cards.'

– *manager Ian Doyle talking about Mike Hallett during the Embassy World Championship.*

'Snooker is not only relaxing – it's educational, requires a lot of concentration, self-control, sportsmanship and precision.'

– *Archbishop Barbarito, Britain's most senior Roman Catholic, talking about the nuns at a Benedictine community in London installing a snooker table in their convent.*

'I remember the World Matchplay between Walter Donaldson and Fred Davis at the Blackpool Tower Circus in 1952. I was working for radio and I was so far back in the crowd that the only way I could tell the difference between the players was that Walter had a bald head.'

– *Ted Lowe, BBC's number 1 snooker commentator, talking about his broadcasting days of years gone by.*

'Please switch off all radio pagers and portable telephones.'

– *an announcement made to the spectators at the Hong Kong Open.*

WHERE THE PLAYERS ARE RANKED AND HOW THEY PICK UP POINTS

The players' world rankings are decided by points scored in specific tournaments over a two-year period. At the time of writing there are expected to be eight ranking tournaments in the 1990/91 season while last season (1989/90) there were ten ranking events.

Five of the tournaments in the 1990/91 season will be staged in the United Kingdom. They are the Rothmans Grand Prix, the StormSeal UK Open, the Mercantile Credit Classic, the Pearl Assurance British Open and the Embassy World Championship. There will be three tournaments overseas: the 555 Asian Open, the Dubai Duty Free Classic and the European Open.

The ranking of each player is calculated on points gained in the preceding two seasons: i.e., the 1990/91 ranking is calculated on points gained in the 1988/89 and 1989/90 seasons. This means that eighteen tournaments will count for ranking positions for the current season.

Many observers feel that snooker would have a much fairer world ranking system if the rankings were updated at the conclusion of each tournament. This would have the backing of many of the players but, unfortunately, the qualifying rounds for these events are held well in advance of the actual competition.

Alternatively, the rankings could be calculated on one year's performance, which would also seem a fairer system and more a testimony of a player's current form.

Ranking points will this year be awarded, with the exception of the World Championship, as follows:

Winner	6 points
Runner-up	5 points
Losing semi-finalist	4 points
Losing quarter-finalist	3 points
Fifth-round loser	2 points
Fourth-round loser	1 point
Third-round loser	1 merit point
Second-round loser	1 'A' point
First-round loser	Frames won in match

The World Championship, understandably, is a special category and higher points are given for this traditional end-of-season tournament. The points awarded in the World Championship are as follows:

Winner	10 points
Runner-up	8 points
Losing semi-finalist	6 points
Losing quarter-finalist	4 points
Second-round loser	2 points
First-round loser	1 ranking point unless member of top sixteen who receives 2 merit points
Fifth-round prelim-round loser	2 merit points
Fourth-round prelim-round loser	1 merit point
Third-round prelim-round loser	1 'A' point
Second-round prelim-round loser	Frames won in match

In the event of ties on ranking points, the player who has picked up most ranking points in the most recent season is allocated a higher placing. If there is still a tie, the player with the greatest number of merit points is given the higher placing. If scores are still equal, the number of merit points in the preceding season applies. In the unlikely event that players are still

Moving up: Neal Foulds who jumped seven places to number 13.

Maltese double act: Joe Grech (left), who finished his first season at number 67, and Tony Drago, the world number 30.

level, their positions are decided on 'A' points, followed by frames won. If, by a remote chance, the players still cannot be separated, their performances in the preceding World Championship will determine their ranking order; and, if this method fails, the other ranking tournaments are worked through in reverse order until the players' positions can be established.

Disappearing act: Alex Higgins who dropped to number 97 after losing 25 world ranking points.

THE OFFICIAL WPBSA WORLD RANKING LIST 1990/91

(1989/90 position in brackets)

POSITION	NAME	R	M	A	F
1 (3)	S. Hendry (Scot)	69	1	–	–
2 (1)	S. Davis (Eng)	67	1	–	–
3 (2)	J. Parrott (Eng)	54	2	–	–
4 (4)	J. White (Eng)	48	2	–	–
5 (10)	D. Mountjoy (Wales)	41	3	–	–
6 (5)	T. Griffiths (Wales)	36	5	–	–
7 (6)	M. Hallett (Eng)	35	4	–	–
8 (15)	D. Reynolds (Eng)	34	2	–	–
9 (16)	S. James (Eng)	32	4	–	–
10 (8)	Dennis Taylor (NI)	29	5	–	–
11 (9)	W. Thorne (Eng)	28	3	–	–
12 (17)	M. Clark (Eng)	27	6	–	–
13 (20)	N. Foulds (Eng)	25	5	–	–
14 (13)	J. Virgo (Eng)	25	4	–	–
15 (14)	A. Meo (Eng)	24	6	–	–
16 (35)	A. Robidoux (Can)	23	4	3	–
17 (11)	J. Johnson (Eng)	23	8	–	–
18 (7)	C. Thorburn (Can)	22	7	–	–
19 (39)	Gary Wilkinson (Eng)	21	4	3	–
20 (19)	S. Newbury (Wales)	21	6	–	–
21 (12)	A. Knowles (Eng)	21	8	–	–
22 (31)	W. Jones (Wales)	19	6	1	–
23 (28)	D. O'Kane (NZ)	18	7	–	–
24 (25)	P. Francisco (SA)	16	11	–	–
25 (29)	R. Chaperon (Can)	16	9	–	–
26 (23)	S. Francisco (SA)	16	10	–	–
27 (21)	B. West (Eng)	16	11	–	–
28 (18)	C. Wilson (Wales)	16	8	1	–
29 (36)	D. Fowler (Eng)	15	10	–	–
30 (30)	A. Drago (Malta)	14	8	–	–
31 (22)	E. Charlton (Aust)	14	8	–	–
32 (–)	J. Wattana (Thai)	12	3	3	–
33 (47)	M. Bennett (Wales)	12	6	4	–
34 (27)	E. Hughes (Rep Ire)	12	9	–	–
35 (62)	A. Jones (Eng)	11	8	5	–
36 (26)	D. Roe (Eng)	11	11	–	–
37 (32)	R. Williams (Eng)	11	12	–	–
38 (–)	N. Bond (Eng)	10	4	2	4
39 (55)	W. King (Aust)	10	7	6	3
40 (53)	D. Morgan (Wales)	10	5	6	–
41 (43)	S. Duggan (Eng)	10	6	4	–
42 (–)	B. Morgan (Eng)	8	2	1	7
43 (41)	A. Chappel (Wales)	8	8	4	–
44 (33)	David Taylor (Eng)	8	11	3	–
45 (65)	L. Dodd (Eng)	7	11	2	5
46 (70)	R. Marshall (Eng)	7	5	5	17
47 (42)	J. Campbell (Aust)	7	6	7	–
48 (48)	C. Roscoe (Wales)	7	4	7	10
49 (58)	J. McLaughlin (NI)	6	11	4	–
50 (59)	I. Graham (Eng)	6	9	5	10
51 (46)	N. Gilbert (Eng)	6	8	7	–
52 (37)	J. Wych (Can)	6	10	3	–
53 (44)	P. Browne (Rep Ire)	6	7	7	–
54 (–)	B. Gollan (Can)	5	2	7	6
55 (38)	J. Spencer (Eng)	5	11	3	–
56 (45)	M. Macleod (Scot)	5	8	5	–
57 (34)	S. Longworth (Eng)	5	9	6	–
58 (60)	J. Chambers (Eng)	4	8	6	2
59 (52)	M. Johnston-Allen (Eng)	4	10	6	–
60 (99)	M. Rowing (Eng)	3	5	4	17
61 (69)	C. Edwards (Eng)	3	4	5	16
62 (40)	J. O'Boye (Eng)	3	8	7	–
63 (79)	B. Rowswell (Eng)	2	5	8	14
64 (–)	N. Dyson (Eng)	2	2	4	11
65 (104)	J. Smith (Eng)	2	2	10	18
66 (82)	P. Gibson (Eng)	2	1	4	11
67 (130)	J. Grech (Malta)	2	7	1	–
68 (50)	K. Stevens (Can)	2	7	9	–
69 (61)	R. Bales (Eng)	2	4	12	–
70 (71)	A. Wilson (Eng)	2	3	7	23
71 (68)	M. Gauvreau (Can)	2	2	13	3
72 (49)	R. Edmonds (Eng)	2	8	9	–
73 (54)	R. Reardon (Wales)	2	5	5	–
74 (63)	D. Gilbert (Eng)	1	9	9	–
75 (57)	T. Murphy (NI)	1	9	8	–
76 (90)	M. Price (Eng)	1	5	5	13
77 (85)	W. Oliver (Eng)	1	6	6	26
78 (80)	P. Medati (Eng)	1	4	4	32
79 (76)	M. Smith (Eng)	1	4	8	17
80 (–)	A. Cairns (Eng)	1	3	3	8
81 (86)	M. Morra (Can)	1	8	3	13
82 (–)	B. Pinches (Eng)	1	2	4	–
83 (–)	I. Brumby (Eng)	1	3	7	–
84 (67)	J. Wright (Eng)	1	2	3	14
85 (66)	John Rea (Scot)	1	8	7	8
86 (72)	N. Terry (Eng)	1	6	5	19
87 (51)	G. Cripsey (Eng)	1	5	12	8
88 (73)	G. Scott (Eng)	1	1	1	26

POSITION	NAME	R	M	A	F
89 (74)	A. Harris (Eng)	1	–	9	37
90 (56)	D. Martin (Eng)	–	10	8	–
91 (98)	S. Campbell (Eng)	–	7	7	22
92 (93)	R. Harris (Eng)	–	6	5	13
93 (94)	E. Sinclair (Scot)	–	6	5	33
94 (78)	G. Miles (Eng)	–	6	6	18
95 (75)	K. Owers (Eng)	–	6	6	14
96 (81)	P. Houlihan (Eng)	–	5	10	6
97 (14)	A. Higgins (NI)	–	5	–	–
98 (–)	S. Murphy (Rep Ire)	–	4	2	12
99 (64)	M. Fisher (Eng)	–	4	14	–
100 (77)	R. Foldvari (Aust)	–	4	5	37
101 (107)	S. Meakin (Eng)	–	3	5	29
102 (114)	P. Watchorn (Rep Ire)	–	2	6	32
103 (92)	I. Williamson (Eng)	–	2	10	22
104 (101)	A. Kearney (Rep Ire)	–	2	8	19
105 (96)	E. Lawlor (Eng)	–	2	8	22
106 (105)	F. Ellis (SA)	–	2	5	29
107 (87)	M. Bradley (Eng)	–	2	10	27
108 (91)	Glen Wilkinson (Aust)	–	2	5	25
109 (–)	D. Campbell (Scot)	–	1	7	4
110 (112)	M. Gibson (Scot)	–	1	7	31
111 (83)	V. Harris (Eng)	–	1	7	23
112 (116)	G. Rigitano (Can)	–	1	6	35
113 (113)	R. Grace (SA)	–	1	6	30
114 (84)	J. Donnelly (Scot)	–	1	3	45
115 (103)	J. van Rensburg (SA)	–	1	3	39
116 (106)	J. Fitzmaurice (Eng)	–	1	8	23
117 (95)	J. Dunning (Eng)	–	1	8	28
118 (100)	T. Whitthread (Eng)	–	1	6	14
119 (88)	J. Bear (Can) (NT)	–	1	5	32
120 (102)	M. Darrington (Eng) (NT)	–	1	5	32
121 (109)	D. Sheehan (Rep Ire) (NT)	–	1	4	41
122 (108)	D. Hughes (Eng) (NT)	–	1	3	25
123 (110)	M. Watterson (Eng) (NT)	–	1	3	32
124 (111)	P. Thornley (Can) (NT)	–	1	–	20
125 (97)	M. Wildman (Eng) (NT)	–	–	7	32
126 (119)	W. Kelly (Rep Ire) (NT)	–	–	7	11
127 (115)	J. Meadowcroft (Eng) (NT)	–	–	6	21
128 (89)	F. Davis (Eng) (NT)	–	–	5	32
129 (118)	G. Foulds (Eng) (NT)	–	–	5	29
130 (120)	G. Jenkins (Aust) (NT)	–	–	3	24
131 (117)	Jack Rea (NI) (NT)	–	–	2	38
132 (122)	B. Mikkelsen (Can) (NT)	–	–	2	20
133 (121)	I. Black (Scot) (NT)	–	–	2	10
134 (132)	C. Everton (Wales) (NT)	–	–	1	3
135 (128)	D. Mienie (SA) (NT)	–	–	1	20
136 (123)	P. Fagan (Rep Ire) (NT)	–	–	1	13
137 (124)	P. Burke (Rep Ire) (NT)	–	–	1	12
138 (129)	J. Rempe (USA) (NT)	–	–	1	12
139 (126)	I. Anderson (Aust) (NT)	–	–	–	7
140 (134)	B. Bennett (Eng) (NT)	–	–	–	4
141 (131)	D. Heaton (Eng) (NT)	–	–	–	3
142 (139)	J. Caggianello (Can) (NT)	–	–	–	–
143 (141)	L. Condo (Aust) (NT)	–	–	–	–
144 (137)	B. Demarco (Scot) (NT)	–	–	–	–
145 (142)	M. Francisco (SA) (NT)	–	–	–	–
146 (148)	S. Frangie (Aust) (NT)	–	–	–	–
147 (143)	J. Giannaros (Aust) (NT)	–	–	–	–
148 (133)	D. Greaves (Eng) (NT)	–	–	–	–
149 (136)	J. Hargreaves (Eng) (NT)	–	–	–	–
150 (140)	M. Hines (SA) (NT)	–	–	–	–
151 (127)	F. Jonik (Can) (NT)	–	–	–	–
152 (138)	E. McLaughlin (Scot) (NT)	–	–	–	–
153 (144)	S. Mizerak (USA) (NT)	–	–	–	–
154 (145)	P. Morgan (Aust) (NT)	–	–	–	–
155 (135)	M. Parkin (Eng) (NT)	–	–	–	–
156 (149)	W. Potasznyk (Aust) (NT)	–	–	–	–
157 (147)	G. Watson (Can) (NT)	–	–	–	–
158 (150)	W. Werbeniuk (Can) (NT)	–	–	–	–

KEY TO TABLE
R – Ranking points
M – Merit points
A – 'A' points
F – Frames won
NT – Non-tournament status

Countries
Aust – Australia
Can – Canada
Eng – England
Malta – Malta
NI – Northern Ireland
NZ – New Zealand
Rep Ire – Republic of Ireland
Scot – Scotland
SA – South Africa
Thai – Thailand
Wales – Wales
USA – United States of America

THE NEW ARRIVALS FOR 1990/91

Snooker will never be the same again after the decision last summer to throw the game 'open'. That historic vote by the players will mean that from the 1991/92 season any player – male or female over the age of sixteen – is eligible to enter any tournament run by the WPBSA.

But to determine the professional line-up for this season, it was 'business as usual' last June with ten amateurs originally due to take on the ten lowest-ranked professionals: the ten winners would have joined the 1990/91 professional circuit. However, two players – world champion Ken Doherty and Jon Birch, the number 1 player at the end of the pro-ticket qualifiers – automatically gained pro status when professionals Paul Thornley of Canada and England's Mark Wildman opted to become non-tournament players for this season. That left thirty-two amateurs fighting it out for eight qualifying places to meet the eight lowest-ranked professionals at the Norbreck Castle Hotel in Blackpool.

All eight professionals lost their matches but there was one note of particular sadness, a moment when snooker thought it had said goodbye to a living legend of the green baize. Fred Davis, OBE, and seventy-six years of age, was beaten 10–5 by Northern Ireland's Jason Prince. Fred, eight times world champion and twice world billiards champion, could have rejoined the circuit in 1991/92; instead he announced his retirement. The brother of Joe Davis, whom many people thought was the greatest player the game has ever seen, said: 'That's it. I will not be playing snooker again. I will continue with billiards, but I will not be playing snooker when the game goes open.' He received a standing ovation from the crowd and then the players as he walked poignantly to the press room for what he thought was his farewell interview.

However, when the WPBSA members voted for 'open' snooker, it was also agreed to make a special category of Life Member for former world professional snooker champions who have attained the age of sixty. Fred fell into that category and, provided his health was good, he was anticipating a return this season in three of the ranking events, including the World Championship.

Now let's take a quick look at the ten new professionals for this season.

KEN DOHERTY

Date of birth: 17 September 1969   *Country:* Republic of Ireland

---

Doherty, the world amateur and world junior champion, had the perfect credentials to join the professional ranks. A Dubliner based in Essex, he is an entertaining player, and such is his potential that he has already signed a five-year contract with Mark McCormack's International Management Group.

JON BIRCH

Date of birth: 15 February 1968   *Country:* England

Birch finished the three-tournament pro-ticket series as number 1 in the rankings and was runner-up to Ken Doherty in the World Amateur Championship in Singapore in 1989. He has a whole string of fine amateur wins to his name.

Fine prospect: Jon Birch.

JASON PRINCE

Date of birth: 17 June 1970   *Country:* Northern Ireland

Prince, a Northern Ireland junior champion, had the unenviable task of playing veteran Fred Davis in the play-offs but came through a 10–5 winner to say: 'I have dreamt of being a professional player since I was six.' Born in Londonderry, he moved to Halifax in Yorkshire three years ago to increase his chances of tougher competitive play. The move has obviously paid off.

The king and the prince: Fred Davis, the one-time king of world snooker, and Jason Prince after Prince had won their pro-ticket play-off match in Blackpool.

CHRIS COOKSON

Date of birth: 25 April 1965   *Country:* England

Cookson, a former sales representative, was the best supported amateur in the play-offs in Blackpool as he lives in nearby Preston. He beat Jim Meadowcroft 10–0 to earn his pro-ticket, while he scored a fine 5–4 win over Scotland's Drew Henry in the previous match.

New boy: Chris Cookson.

JASON FERGUSON

Date of birth: 31 May 1969   *Country:* England

Ferguson, from Mansfield, nearly failed at the final hurdle of his battle to become a professional when he trailed Irish pro Billy Kelly 7–5. However, watched by his parents, he took the final five frames for a 10–5 victory, finishing the match off with a break of 79.

ROD LAWLER

Date of birth: 12 July 1971   *Country:* England

Lawler, the British under-19 champion from Liverpool, started playing as a thirteen-year-old when he went with his parents to Butlin's Holiday Camp in Pwllheli. He was only eighteen when he beat Mike Watterson 10–1 to earn his professional ticket. It was an impressive performance with seven breaks of more than 40.

Cueing up: Liverpool's Rod Lawler.

ALAN McMANUS

Date of birth: 21 January 1971   *Country:* Scotland

Glaswegian McManus enjoyed a remarkable 1989/90 season as he became number 1 in the Scottish amateur rankings, won the Scottish Championship, finished runner-up in the BCE English Championship and earned his professional place by beating Dennis Hughes 10–1. Just for good measure he helped Scotland win the Home International Championship. During his win over Hughes he included nine breaks of more than 40.

JASON WHITTAKER

Date of birth: 31 January 1972   *Country:* England

Whittaker, at eighteen years and four months, was the youngest new professional when he beat Ireland's Dessie Sheehan 10–2 in Blackpool. Born in Morecambe, Lancashire, and now based in Torquay, he is a talented young player.

FRANKY CHAN

Date of birth: 21 February 1965   *Country:* Hong Kong

Chan was one of four overseas players given a special invitation to play in the pro-ticket play-offs in Blackpool. This snooker hall manager beat two amateurs and then English professional Mike Darrington 10–7 to seal his place in the pro ranks. A world amateur semi-finalist, Chan started playing as a twelve-year-old when a small table was installed in his school!

Star from the Orient: Franky Chan.

GARY NATALE

Date of birth: 24 April 1962   *Country:* Canada

Natale, from Toronto, plays at the Blues and Cues Club in his home town and only returned to the sport when he was twenty-one after a seven-year lay-off. Natale was persuaded to start playing again by a friend and won the Canadian Championship in 1986. He beat fellow Canadian Jim Bear 10–6 to collect his pro-ticket and was the only player to score a century – a 105 – in the play-offs.

	Lion Brown Masters	Hong Kong Open	555 Asian Open	Regal Masters	BCE International	Rothmans Grand Prix	Dubai Duty Free Classic	StormSeal UK Open	Norwich Union European Grand Prix	Everest World Matchplay
1 S. Hendry	4,230.77	6,000	40,000 2,500 (HB)	32,500	24,000	5,250	40,000 2,500 (HB)	100,000 2,000 (HB)	10,000	20,000 10,000 (HB)
2 S. Davis				8,000	40,000	70,000		48,000 8,000 (HB)		10,000
3 J. White		12,000	500	3,750	6,000	5,250 3,500 (HB)		12,000		100,000
4 J. Parrott	3,461.54	2,500		8,000 3,500 (HB)	6,000 4,000 (HB)	5,250	12,000	6,000	5,000	40,000
5 S. James		2,500	2,500		3,000	1,531.25	3,750	1,750		
6 T. Griffiths		2,500	12,000	16,000	1,937.50	1,531.25		24,000		10,000
7 D. Mountjoy		3,750	3,750		875	10,500	22,500	1,750	2,500	10,000
8 Dennis Taylor	3,461.54	6,000	500	1,500	3,000	10,500		6,000		10,000
9 M. Hallett	3,461.54	40,000 1,000 (HB)	2,500	3,750	1,937.50	3,390.62	500	12,000	2,500	5,000
10 R. Chaperon		2,500	500		1,937.50	1,531.25	500	3,875		
11 W. Thorne	11,538.46 961.54 (HB)	3,750	6,000		3,000	3,390.62 1,750 (HB)		6,000		5,000
12 A. Higgins		3,750	2,500		875	3,390.62	6,000	3,875		
13 D. Reynolds		500	2,500		875	42,000	6,000	6,000		20,000
14 J. Johnson	7,692.31	500	2,500		875	10,500 3,500 (HB)	500	6,000	20,000	
15 A. Meo		2,500	2,500		875	3,390.62		1,750		5,000
16 C. Thorburn		500	500	3,750	875	3,390.62		3,875		5,000
17 N. Foulds		6,000	2,500		3,000	3,390.62		3,875		
18 A. Robidoux		2,500			12,000	5,250	2,500	12,000		
19 Gary Wilkinson		12,000	12,000			3,390.62	2,500	24,000		
20 J. Wattana			22,500		1,937.50	21,000	2,500	1,750		
21 A. Knowles	5,000	500	3,750		3,000	10,500	500	6,000	5,000	
22 D. O'Kane	3,461.54	22,500 2,500 (HB)	2,500		875	1,531.25	2,500	3,875		
23 W. King		500	2,500		875	3,390.62	2,500	1,750		
24 M. Clark		3,750	6,000 1,000 (HB)		1,937.50	3,390.62	3,750	3,875	2,500	
25 D. Fowler		500	500			21,000	12,000	1,750		
26 J. Virgo		3,750	3,750		875	3,390.62	3,750	1,750	2,500	
27 D. Morgan			500		875	1,531.25	500			
28 S. Newbury		3,750	500		3,000	5,250	500	1,750		
29 S. Francisco		500	6,000		1,937.50	1,531.25	500	3,875		
30 W. Jones		2,500	3,750		1,937.50	1,531.25	2,500	3,875		
31 P. Francisco		500	3,750		875	1,531.25	6,000	6,000		
32 A. Drago		500	3,750		1,937.50	1,531.25	3,750	3,875		
33 N. Bond		500			12,000	3,390.62	3,750	1,750		
34 M. Bennett			500		1,937.50	1,531.25	500	12,000		
35 R. Marshall			500		3,000		500	1,750		
36 C. Wilson		2,500	500		6,000	1,531.25	2,500	3,875		
37 E. Charlton		2,500	500		1,937.50	1,531.25	2,500	1,750		
38 E. Hughes		500	2,500		1,937.50	3,390.62	500	1,750		
39 A. Jones		3,750	6,000		3,000	5,250	2,500	3,875		
40 B. West		2,500	3,750		1,937.50	1,531.25	3,750	3,875		
41 B. Morgan		2,500			6,000		500	3,875		
42 D. Roe		2,500	2,500		875	1,531.25	3,750	1,750		
43 L. Dodd		3,750			875	3,390.62	500			
44 A. Chappel			500				2,500 1,000 (HB)	1,750		
45 R. Williams		500	500		875	1,531.25	500	3,875		
46 T. Murphy					875			1,750		
47 J. Campbell					875	1,531.25	2,500			
48 B. Gollan		2,500	2,500		875			6,000		
49 I. Graham		6,000	2,500		875			1,750		
50 J. Chambers		2,500	500			3,390.62	2,500	1,750		
51 S. Duggan		500	3,750		875	1,531.25		1,750		
52 J. McLaughlin		500	500		875	1,531.25	6,000	1,750		
53 P. Browne			500				500	1,750		
54 M. Macleod		500		1,500	875		500			
55 N. Gilbert						1,531.25				
56 M. Johnston-Allen			500		1,937.50	1,531.25		1,750		
57 C. Roscoe		500	2,500			1,531.25				
58 M. Rowing		500						1,750		
59 David Taylor		500	500				500	1,750		
60 D. Gilbert		500	2,500			1,531.25		1,750		

THE MONEY GO?

Mercantile Credit Classic	European Open	Benson and Hedges Masters	Senator Windows	Pearl Assurance British Open	Professional Players Tournament	British Car Rental World Cup	Benson and Hedges Irish Masters	Continental Airlines London Masters	Leagues (StormSeal and International)	Embassy World Championship	TOTAL (£)
2,906.25	22,500	70,000 3,500 (HB)		1,640		3,000	8,186.99	30,000	30,000	120,000	590,714.01
18,000	12,000	21,000 3,500 (HB)		5,625 1,876 (HB)		3,000	35,637.49	3,500	78,000	36,000	402,138.49
	3,750	21,000		5,625 7,500 (HB)		3,000	14,447.63	3,500	25,000 4,000 (HB)	72,000	302,822.63
4,500	40,000	38,000		1,640		3,000	8,186.99 1,926.35 (HB)	12,500 3,500 (HB)	5,000 5,000 (HB)	36,000 12,000 (HB)	266,964.88
60,000 6,000 (HB)	12,000 2,500 (HB)	7,000		22,500						9,000	134,031.25
1,312.50	500	7,000	900	3,634		3,000	14,447.63		10,000	18,000	126,762.88
1,312.50	6,000	13,000	6,000	5,625		3,000	5,297.47		20,000	9,000	124,859.97
2,906.25	500	7,000		5,625		10,000	22,153.04	3,500	17,000	5,000	114,645.83
2,906.25	500	7,000		3,634			5,297.47	3,500	6,000	9,000	113,877.38
2,906.25	2,500			75,000		16,000 2,000 (HB)				4,000	113,250.00
1,312.50	2,500	13,000		1,640			8,186.99 1,926.35 (HB)	7,500	25,000	9,000	111,456.46
2,906.25	2,500	5,000		45,000		10,000	8,186.99		5,000	5,000	103,983.86
2,906.25	2,500	5,000		3,634						9,000	100,915.25
1,312.50	3,750	13,000		3,634			5,297.47			5,000	84,061.28
2,906.25	500	7,000		3,634				7,500	36,000	9,000	82,555.87
2,906.25	500	7,000		1,640		16,000 2,000 (HB)	5,297.47		9,000	18,000	80,234.34
1,312.50	6,000			11,250					15,000	18,000	70,328.12
	2,500			5,625		16,000 2,000 (HB)				5,000	65,375.00
4,500				1,640						5,000	65,030.62
		7,000		3,634						4,000	64,321.50
1,312.50	500	13,000		5,625						9,000	63,687.50
9,000	2,500			1,640		3,000				4,000	59,882.79
36,000					150	5,000				400	53,065.62
4,500	2,500			11,250						4,000	48,453.12
1,312.50	2,500			1,640	600					5,000	46,802.50
4,500	2,500	7,000		1,640						9,000	44,405.62
4,500	500		10,500 1,200 (HB)	3,634	2,650					18,000	44,390.25
9,000	2,500		900	11,250	600					5,000	44,000.00
18,000	2,500			1,640		3,000				4,000	43,483.75
9,000	2,500		2,750	1,640						5,000	36,983.75
4,500	500			5,625	400					5,000	34,681.25
4,500	500			3,634	600 500 (HB)	3,000				5,000	33,077.75
	6,000				750					4,000	32,140.62
1,312.50	3,750		350	3,634	1,200					5,000	31,715.25
				22,500	250					2,062.50	30,562.50
1,312.50	500		900	1,640		3,000				5,000	29,258.75
2,906.25	3,750			1,640		5,000				5,000	29,015.00
1,312.50	500			5,625	550	5,000				4,000	27,565.62
1,312.50										400	26,087.50
1,312.50	500			1,640						4,000	24,796.25
9,000										2,062.50	23,937.50
1,312.50	2,500			1,640	275					4,000	22,633.75
				11,250	400					2,062.50	22,228.12
1,312.50	3,750		2,750	1,640	1,800					5,000	22,002.50
2,906.25	2,500			3,634						4,000	20,821.50
1,312.50 1,500 (HB)				3,634	425	10,000				400	19,896.50
2,906.25	3,750				550	5,000				2,062.50	19,175.00
				1,640						5,000	18,515.00
	500			1,640	150					4,000	17,415.00
1,312.50	500									4,000	16,453.12
2,906.25				3,634	525					400	15,871.50
2,906.25	500				750					400	15,712.50
	500			3,634	400	5,000				2,062.50	14,346.50
1,312.50				3,634	300	3,000				2,062.50	13,684.00
2,906.25	500				425					5,000 3,000 (HB)	13,362.50
1,312.50	500			1,640	150					4,000	13,321.25
1,312.50	6,000		350							400	12,593.75
4,500				3,634						2,062.50	12,446.50
2,906.25	2,500			1,640	1,350					400	12,046.25
					2,650					2.062.50	10,993.75

	Lion Brown Masters	Hong Kong Open	555 Asian Open	Regal Masters	BCE International	Rothmans Grand Prix	Dubai Duty Free Classic	StormSeal UK Open	Norwich Union European Grand Prix	Everest World Matchplay
61 John Rea		500	500	3,750						
62 M. Price		500	500					1,750		
63 J. Wych		500	500		875 / 1,000 (HB)	1,531.25	2,500			
64 B. Rowswell						3,390.62	2,500	1,750		
65 J. Spencer		500	500				2,500	1,750		
66 A. Wilson										
67 S. Campbell			500			1,531.25		1,750		
68 A. Cairns			500		1,937.50					
69 N. Terry			500				500	1,750		
70 N. Dyson					875					
71 C. Edwards			500							
72 W. Oliver			2,500			1,531.25				
73 J. Smith					875	5,250				
74 J. O'Boye			500		875		500	3,875		
75 A. Kearney					875					
76 E. Sinclair						1,531.25	500			
77 P. Gibson						5,250	500			
78 R. Foldvari		500								
79 S. Longworth						1,531.25	500	1,750		
80 K. Owers										
81 R. Bales		500			1,937.50			500		
82 J. Wright		500			875			500		
83 K. Stevens								3,875		
84 S. Murphy						1,531.25				
85 B. Pinches		2,500								
86 R. Edmonds		500				1,531.25				
87 R. Harris			500		875			500		
88 I. Brumby		500			875					
89 G. Miles			500					500		
90 P. Medati							2,500	1,750		
91 M. Morra						3,390.62		500		
92 J. Grech								3,750		
93 M. Gauvreau		2,500						500		
94 S. Meakin						1,531.25		1,750		
95 P. Watchorn										
96 P. Houlihan		500			875					
97 G. Cripsey			500			1,531.25				
98 D. Martin		500	500					500		
99 M. Smith					1,937.50					
100 V. Harris						1,531.25				
101 J. Donnelly										
102 M. Fisher					875			500		
103 I. Williamson					875					
104 D. Campbell										
105 R. Reardon										
106 G. Rigitano		500								
107 M. Gibson		500								
108 R. Grace										
109 E. Lawlor								500		
110 A. Harris										
111 F. Ellis										
112 G. Scott								500		
113 D. Hughes										
114 J. Dunning										
115 J. Fitzmaurice										
116 J. van Rensburg								500		
117 Glen Wilkinson										
118 J. Bear										
119 M. Bradley										
120 M. Darrington										
121 T. Whitthread										
122 M. Wildman										
123 P. Burke										
124 F. Davis										
125 G. Jenkins										
126 D. Mienie										
127 Jack Rea										
128 D. Sheehan										
129 P. Thornley										
130 M. Watterson										
131 I. Black										
132 B. Mikkelsen										
133 B. Bennett										

Mercantile Credit Classic	European Open	Benson and Hedges Masters	Senator Windows	Pearl Assurance British Open	Professional Players Tournament	British Car Rental World Cup	Benson and Hedges Irish Masters	Continental Airlines London Masters	Leagues (StormSeal and International)	Embassy World Championship	TOTAL (£)
					750	3,000				2,062.50	10,562.50
	2,500				1,000					4,000	10,250.00
1,312.50				1,640							9,858.75
1,312.50					400					250	9,603.12
	500			1,640						2,062.50	9,452.50
				3,634	550					4,000	8,184.00
										4,000	7,781.25
1,312,50					1,350					2,062.50	7,162.50
1,312.50				1,640						400	7,102.50
	1,000 (HB)										
1,312.50	3,750				675					400	7,012.50
1,312.50	3,750				875					400	6,837.50
	500			1,640	400					250	6,821.25
					400					250	6,775.00
	500									400	6,650.00
					300	5,000				400	6,575.00
1,312.50	500			1,640	425					400	6,308.75
					300					250	6,300.00
	500				5,000					250	6,250.00
				1,640	400					400	6,221.25
	500				5,250					400	6,150.00
	500			1,640	650					400	6,127.50
1,312.50	500			1,640	425					250	6,002.50
				1,640						400	5,915.00
1,312.50	500			1,640	550					250	5,783.75
	500				400					2,062.50	5,462.50
1,312.50										2,062.50	5,406.25
1,312.50				1,640	150					400	5,377.50
2,906.25					675					400	5,356.25
				1,640	400					2,062.50	5,102.50
					275					250	4,775.00
										400	4,290.62
											3,750.00
					150					400	3,550.00
										250	3,531.25
1,312.50					150					2,062.50	3,525.00
										2,062.50	3,437.50
					650					400	3,081.25
	500				425					400	2,825.00
					425					400	2,762.50
					525					250	2,306.25
				1,640	400					250	2,290.00
					150					400	1,925.00
					550					250	1,675.00
	500				400					400	1,300.00
			900							400	1,300.00
					400					400	1,300.00
					300					250	1,050.00
	500									400	900.00
										400	900.00
					525					250	775.00
	500									250	750.00
										250	750.00
					300					250	550.00
					275					250	525.00
					250					250	500.00
											500.00
										250	500.00
										400	400.00
					150					250	400.00
					150					250	400.00
					150					250	400.00
					150					250	400.00
					250						250.00
										250	250.00
										250	250.00
										250	250.00
										250	250.00
										250	250.00
										250	250.00
										250	250.00
										250	250.00
					150						150.00
					150						150.00
					50						50.00

THE TOP THIRTY-TWO: BEST PERFORMANCES AND WHO WON WHAT WHERE AND WHEN

STEPHEN HENDRY

World ranking: Number 1
Date of birth: 13 January 1969
Star sign: Capricorn

Prize money 1989/90: £590,714.01
Turned professional: 1985
Country: Scotland

Stephen Hendry will never forget the 1989/90 season as it was the one in which he achieved his dream of becoming the world number 1 and the youngest world champion in the history of the game. It was a remarkable performance by a young man who went on to win seven major titles and £590,714.01 in prize money. Hendry won the 555 Asian Open, the Dubai Duty Free Classic, the StormSeal UK Open, the Regal Masters, the Benson and Hedges Masters, the Continental Airlines London Masters and the Embassy World Championship; and he finished runner-up in the StormSeal Matchroom League. The climax of his remarkable season came at the Crucible Theatre in Sheffield when he beat Jimmy White 18–12 in the final of the Embassy World Championship. Hendry, who was twenty-one years and three months of age, became the youngest world champion, beating Alex Higgins' previous record of twenty-two years and eleven months. Hendry is already one of the richest young men in British sport and he owns property in Scotland worth more than £½ million. He seems certain to dominate professional snooker for many years.

Taking it easy: world number 1 Stephen Hendry.

BEST PERFORMANCES

Embassy World Championship:
Winner 1990 (beat Jimmy White 18–12)

Other Ranking Tournaments
Hong Kong Open:
Quarter-finalist 1989 (lost to Mike Hallett 5–4)
555 Asian Open:
Winner 1989 (beat James Wattana 9–6)
BCE International:
Runner-up 1989 (lost to Steve Davis 9–4)
Rothmans Grand Prix:
Winner 1987 (beat Dennis Taylor 10–7)
Dubai Duty Free Classic:
Winner 1989 (beat Doug Mountjoy 9–2)
StormSeal UK Open:
Winner 1989 (beat Steve Davis 16–12)
Mercantile Credit Classic:
Semi-finalist 1987 (lost to Steve Davis 9–3)
Pearl Assurance British Open:
Winner 1988 (beat Mike Hallett 13–2)
European Open:
Runner-up 1990 (lost to John Parrott 10–6)

Current Non-ranking Tournaments
Benson and Hedges Masters:
Winner 1989 (beat John Parrott 9–6)
Winner 1990 (beat John Parrott 9–4)
Benson and Hedges Irish Masters:
Runner-up 1989 (lost to Alex Higgins 9–8)
Everest World Matchplay:
Semi-finalist 1988 (lost to John Parrott 9–5)
Semi-finalist 1989 (lost to John Parrott 9–8)
Regal Masters:
Winner 1989 (beat Terry Griffiths 10–1)

Other Wins
British Isles Under-16: 1983
Scottish Amateur: 1984, 1985
Scottish Professional: 1986, 1987, 1988
Winfield Masters: 1987
Foster's World Doubles: 1987
Lion Brown New Zealand Masters: 1988
Continental Airlines London Masters: 1989, 1990
Pontin's Professional: 1990

World Ranking Positions

1986/87	51	1988/89	4	1990/91	1
1987/88	23	1989/90	3		

STEVE DAVIS

World ranking: Number 2
Date of birth: 22 August 1957
Star sign: Leo

Prize money 1989/90: £402,138.49
Turned professional: 1978
Country: England

Steve Davis, the Essex superstar who dominated the 1980s by winning fifty major titles, including the World Championship on six occasions, begins the new decade as the world number 2. It's the first time that he has not occupied the number 1 position since he took over the top spot in 1983. He also lost his world title when he was beaten 16–14 by Jimmy White in the semi-final. But Davis is determined to regain his number 1 placing and has this season decided to enter all the ranking tournaments. Last season he opted out of three overseas events which cost him dearly in the chase for ranking points. Despite the disappointments, he still collected two ranking tournament titles – the BCE International and the Rothmans Grand Prix – and also won the StormSeal Matchroom League for the fourth successive year and the Benson and Hedges Irish Masters for the fifth time. Davis was married last summer to Judy Greig and the couple live in a small Essex village.

Determined: Steve Davis who will this season be aiming to regain his world title and world number 1 ranking.

BEST PERFORMANCES

Embassy World Championship:
Winner 1981 (beat Doug Mountjoy 18–12)
Winner 1983 (beat Cliff Thorburn 18–6)
Winner 1984 (beat Jimmy White 18–16)
Winner 1987 (beat Joe Johnson 18–14)
Winner 1988 (beat Terry Griffiths 18–11)
Winner 1989 (beat John Parrott 18–3)

Other Ranking Tournaments

Hong Kong Open:
Did not enter
555 Asian Open:
Did not enter
BCE International:
Winner 1983 (beat Cliff Thorburn 9–4)
Winner 1984 (beat Tony Knowles 9–2)
Winner 1987 (beat Cliff Thorburn 12–5)
Winner 1988 (beat Jimmy White 12–6)
Winner 1989 (beat Stephen Hendry 9–4)
Rothmans Grand Prix:
Winner 1985 (beat Dennis Taylor 10–9)
Winner 1988 (beat Alex Higgins 10–6)
Winner 1989 (beat Dean Reynolds 10–0)
Dubai Duty Free Classic:
Did not enter
StormSeal UK Open:
Winner 1984 (beat Alex Higgins 16–8)
Winner 1985 (beat Willie Thorne 16–14)
Winner 1986 (beat Neal Foulds 16–7)
Winner 1987 (beat Jimmy White 16–14)
Mercantile Credit Classic:
Winner 1984 (beat Tony Meo 9–8)
Winner 1987 (beat Jimmy White 13–12)
Winner 1988 (beat John Parrott 13–11)
Pearl Assurance British Open:
Winner 1986 (beat Willie Thorne 12–7)
European Open:
Semi-finalist 1990 (lost to Stephen Hendry 6–3)

Current Non-ranking Tournaments

Benson and Hedges Masters:
Winner 1982 (beat Terry Griffiths 9–5)
Winner 1988 (beat Mike Hallett 9–0)
Benson and Hedges Irish Masters:
Winner 1983 (beat Ray Reardon 9–2)
Winner 1984 (beat Terry Griffiths 9–1)
Winner 1987 (beat Willie Thorne 9–1)
Winner 1988 (beat Neal Foulds 9–4)
Winner 1990 (beat Dennis Taylor 9–4)
Everest World Matchplay:
Winner 1988 (beat John Parrott 9–5)
Regal Masters:
Semi-finalist 1989 (lost to Terry Griffiths 6–2)

Other Wins

Pontin's Open: 1978, 1979
Coral UK: 1980, 1981
Lada Classic: 1981 (played December 1980)
English Professional: 1981, 1985
Yamaha International Masters: 1981, 1982, 1984
Jameson International: 1981
Pot Black: 1982, 1983
Pontin's Professional: 1982
Tolly Cobbold Classic: 1982, 1983, 1984
Winfield Masters: 1982
Langs Supreme Masters: 1982, 1983, 1984
Hofmeister World Doubles: 1982, 1983, 1985, 1986
Camus Hong Kong Masters: 1984
Riley Hong Kong Masters: 1987
Camus Singapore Masters: 1985
BCE Canadian Masters: 1986
Brazilian Masters: 1986
Camus China Masters: 1986
Matchroom League: 1987, 1988, 1989, 1990
LEP Matchroom League: 1988
Fersina Windows World Cup: 1981, 1983, 1988, 1989
Norwich Union Grand Prix: 1988
Hong Kong Gold Cup: 1989

World Ranking Positions

1980/81	13	1984/85	1	1987/88	1
1981/82	2	1985/86	1	1988/89	1
1982/83	4	1986/87	1	1989/90	1
1983/84	1			1990/91	2

JOHN PARROTT

World ranking: Number 3
Date of birth: 11 May 1964
Star sign: Taurus

Prize money 1989/90: £266,964.88
Turned professional: 1983
Country: England

John Parrott, who dropped one place in the rankings to number 3, retained his European title in Lyon, France, when he beat Stephen Hendry 10–6 after one of the best performances of his career. He also reached three other finals – the Benson and

Hedges Masters, the Everest World Matchplay and the Continental Airlines London Masters – but lost to Hendry (twice) and Jimmy White. Parrott had the distinction of scoring the highest professional break of the season – a 142 against Hendry in the StormSeal Matchroom League. Unfortunately, he was also relegated from the League. Last season saw a major change in the direction of Parrott's career when he decided to leave the Scottish-based Cuemasters squad and return full-time to manager Phil Miller.

Euro champ: John Parrott celebrates with wife Karen after he retained his European Open title.

BEST PERFORMANCES

Embassy World Championship:
Runner-up 1989 (lost to Steve Davis 18–3)

Other Ranking Tournaments
Hong Kong Open:
Round 4 1989 (lost to Steve Newbury 5–2)
555 Asian Open:
Round 3 1989 (withdrew)
BCE International:
Quarter-finalist 1985 (lost to Dennis Taylor 5–1)
Quarter-finalist 1989 (lost to Nigel Bond 5–2)
Rothmans Grand Prix:
Semi-finalist 1987 (lost to Stephen Hendry 9–7)
Dubai Duty Free Classic:
Semi-finalist 1989 (lost to Doug Mountjoy 5–4)
StormSeal UK Open:
Semi-finalist 1986 (lost to Neal Foulds 9–3)
Mercantile Credit Classic:
Runner-up 1988 (lost to Steve Davis 13–11)
Pearl Assurance British Open:
Semi-finalist 1988 (lost to Mike Hallett 9–8)
Semi-finalist 1989 (lost to Dean Reynolds 9–8)
European Open:
Winner 1989 (beat Terry Griffiths 9–5)
Winner 1990 (beat Stephen Hendry 10–6)

Current Non-ranking Tournaments
Benson and Hedges Masters:
Runner-up 1989 (lost to Stephen Hendry 9–6)
Runner-up 1990 (lost to Stephen Hendry 9–4)
Benson and Hedges Irish Masters:
Semi-finalist 1989 (lost to Alex Higgins 6–4)
Everest World Matchplay:
Runner-up 1988 (lost to Steve Davis 9–5)
Runner-up 1989 (lost to Jimmy White 18–9)
Regal Masters:
Semi-finalist 1989 (lost to Stephen Hendry 6–4)

Other Wins
Junior Pot Black: 1982, 1983
Pontin's Open: 1982, 1986
Pontin's Professional: 1988
Kent China Cup: 1988

World Ranking Positions

Season	Position	Season	Position
1984/85	20	1988/89	7
1985/86	18	1989/90	2
1986/87	17	1990/91	3
1987/88	13		

JIMMY WHITE

World ranking: Number 4
Date of birth: 2 May 1962
Star sign: Taurus

Prize money 1989/90: £302,822.63
Turned professional: 1980
Country: England

Jimmy White finished the season as the Everest World Matchplay champion and was one victory away from the greatest prize of all in the Embassy World Championship. He captured the Matchplay with an outstanding 18–9 defeat of John Parrott and reached the world final with a breathtaking 16–14 victory over Steve Davis, the defending champion. But White failed to get over the final hurdle as he lost 18–12 to Stephen Hendry – the second time that he had been denied the world title. This talented left-hander from London still remains one of the most popular players in the game. At home, wife Maureen presented White with their fourth daughter, whom they called Cassandra.

WHO SAID THAT?

'Everybody seems to be talking about Stephen Hendry and Steve Davis. It needles me when some people want to write me off.'

▲

– Jimmy White.

Status quo: Jimmy White who started and finished the season at number 4.

BEST PERFORMANCES

Embassy World Championship:
Runner-up 1984 (lost to Steve Davis 18–16)
Runner-up 1990 (lost to Stephen Hendry 18–12)

Other Ranking Tournaments
Hong Kong Open:
Semi-finalist 1989 (lost to Mike Hallett 5–2)
555 Asian Open:
Round 3 1989 (lost to Colin Roscoe 5–3)
BCE International:
Runner-up 1985 (lost to Cliff Thorburn 12–10)
Runner-up 1988 (lost to Steve Davis 12–6)

Rothmans Grand Prix:
Winner 1986 (beat Rex Williams 10–6)
Dubai Duty Free Classic:
Did not enter
StormSeal UK Open:
Runner-up 1987 (lost to Steve Davis 16–14)
Mercantile Credit Classic:
Winner 1986 (beat Cliff Thorburn 13–12)
Pearl Assurance British Open:
Winner 1987 (beat Neal Foulds 13–9)
European Open:
Semi-finalist 1989 (lost to Terry Griffiths 5–4)

Current Non-ranking Tournaments
Benson and Hedges Masters:
Winner 1984 (beat Terry Griffiths 9–5)
Benson and Hedges Irish Masters:
Winner 1985 (beat Alex Higgins 9–5)
Winner 1986 (beat Willie Thorne 9–5)
Everest World Matchplay:
Winner 1989 (beat John Parrott 18–9)
Regal Masters:
Quarter-finalist 1989 (lost to Terry Griffiths 6–3)

Other Wins
British Isles Under-16: 1977
Pontin's Autumn Open: 1978

English Amateur: 1979
World Amateur: 1980
Indian Amateur: 1980
Langs Supreme Masters: 1981
Northern Ireland Classic: 1981
Hofmeister World Doubles: 1984
Carlsberg Challenge: 1984, 1985
Pot Black: 1986
Camus Malaysian Masters: 1986
Fersina Windows World Cup: 1988, 1989
LEP Hong Kong Masters: 1988
BCE Canadian Masters: 1988

World Ranking Positions

1981/82	21	1984/85	7	1988/89	2
1982/83	10	1985/86	7	1989/90	4
1983/84	11	1986/87	5	1990/91	4
		1987/88	2		

DOUG MOUNTJOY

World ranking: Number 5
Date of birth: 8 June 1942
Star sign: Gemini

Prize money 1989/90: £124,859.97
Turned professional: 1976
Country: Wales

Still moving up: Doug Mountjoy jumped five places to number 5 in the world rankings.

Doug Mountjoy didn't win any titles last season but still jumped five places up the rankings from number 10 to number 5. That completed a remarkable rise of nineteen places in just two seasons under the guidance of top coach Frank Callan. Mountjoy's best performance in a ranking tournament came in the Dubai Duty Free Classic where he picked up five points after losing 9–2 to Stephen Hendry in the final.

The second half of the season proved a slight disappointment, especially when he lost his Senator Windows Welsh Championship title to Darren Morgan. In the World Championship Mountjoy came through the first round 10–8 against Canadian Brady Gollan, but then went out 13–12 to another Canadian, Cliff Thorburn, in the longest match of the tournament.

BEST PERFORMANCES

Embassy World Championship:
Runner-up 1981 (lost to Steve Davis 18–12)

Other Ranking Tournaments
Hong Kong Open:
Round 5 1989 (lost to Jimmy White 5–3)
555 Asian Open:
Round 5 1989 (lost to James Wattana 5–2)
BCE International:
Quarter-finalist 1983 (lost to Cliff Thorburn 5–2)
Rothmans Grand Prix:
Quarter-finalist 1984 (lost to Cliff Thorburn 5–3)
Quarter-finalist 1989 (lost to James Wattana 5–2)
Dubai Duty Free Classic:
Runner-up 1989 (lost to Stephen Hendry 9–2)
StormSeal UK Open:
Winner 1988 (beat Stephen Hendry 16–12)
Mercantile Credit Classic:
Winner 1989 (beat Wayne Jones 13–11)
Pearl Assurance British Open:
Round 5 1987 (lost to Cliff Thorburn 5–4)
Round 5 1989 (lost to John Parrott 5–2)
Round 5 1990 (lost to Alex Higgins 5–3)
European Open:
Quarter-finalist 1990 (lost to Steve Davis 5–0)

Current Non-ranking Tournaments
Benson and Hedges Masters:
Winner 1977 (beat Ray Reardon 7–6)
Benson and Hedges Irish Masters:
Winner 1979 (beat Ray Reardon 6–5)
Everest World Matchplay:
Quarter-finalist 1989 (lost to Jimmy White 9–5)

Other Wins
Welsh Amateur: 1968, 1976
World Amateur: 1976
Pontin's Open: 1974, 1976
Pot Black: 1978, 1985
Coral UK: 1978
Pontin's Professional: 1979, 1983
State Express World Cup: 1979, 1980
Champion of Champions: 1980
Welsh Professional: 1980, 1982, 1984, 1987, 1989
Camus Hong Kong Masters: 1983

World Ranking Positions

1977/78	14	1982/83	7	1986/87	14
1978/79	14	1983/84	12	1987/88	14
1979/80	13	1984/85	15	1988/89	24
1980/81	14	1985/86	15	1989/90	10
1981/82	6			1990/91	5

TERRY GRIFFITHS

World ranking: Number 6
Date of birth: 16 October 1947
Star sign: Libra

Prize money 1989/90: £126,762.88
Turned professional: 1978
Country: Wales

Terry Griffiths didn't enjoy one of his better seasons, although he only dropped one place down the rankings to number 6. He reached the semi-finals of the 555 Asian Open and the StormSeal UK Open and also the quarter-final of the World Championship where he was beaten 13–5 by Jimmy White. Away from the ranking tournaments, Griffiths was a finalist in the inaugural Regal Scottish Masters in Glasgow, but was hammered 10–1 by Stephen Hendry. Griffiths is a devoted family man and also owns a luxury snooker club in his native Llanelli.

Slight slip: Terry Griffiths who dropped one place to number 6.

BEST PERFORMANCES

Embassy World Championship:
Winner 1979 (beat Dennis Taylor 24–16)

Other Ranking Tournaments
Hong Kong Open:
Round 4 1989 (lost to Dene O'Kane 5–4)
555 Asian Open:
Semi-finalist 1989 (lost to James Wattana 5–0)
BCE International:
Semi-finalist 1983 (lost to Cliff Thorburn 9–8)
Rothmans Grand Prix:
Quarter-finalist 1982 (lost to Jimmy White 5–2)
Quarter-finalist 1985 (lost to Cliff Thorburn 5–1)
Dubai Duty Free Classic:
Did not enter
StormSeal UK Open:
Semi-finalist 1988 (lost to Doug Mountjoy 9–4)
Semi-finalist 1989 (lost to Stephen Hendry 9–7)
Mercantile Credit Classic:
Quarter-finalist 1984 (lost to Steve Davis 5–4)
Quarter-finalist 1985 (lost to Cliff Thorburn 5–4)
Quarter-finalist 1987 (lost to Jimmy White 5–3)
Quarter-finalist 1988 (lost to Steve Newbury 5–4)
Pearl Assurance British Open:
Quarter-finalist 1986 (lost to Willie Thorne 5–4)
European Open:
Runner-up 1989 (lost to John Parrott 9–8)

Current Non-ranking Tournaments
Benson and Hedges Masters:
Winner 1980 (beat Alex Higgins 9–5)
Benson and Hedges Irish Masters:
Winner 1980 (beat Doug Mountjoy 9–8)
Winner 1981 (beat Ray Reardon 9–7)
Winner 1982 (beat Steve Davis 9–5)
Everest World Matchplay:
Quarter-finalist 1988 (lost to Jimmy White 9–5)
Quarter-finalist 1989 (lost to Stephen Hendry 9–3)
Regal Masters:
Runner-up 1989 (lost to Stephen Hendry 10–1)

Other Wins
Welsh Amateur: 1975
English Amateur: 1977, 1978
State Express World Cup: 1979, 1980
Pontin's Professional: 1981, 1985, 1986
Coral UK: 1982
Lada Classic: 1982
Pontin's Open: 1983
Pot Black: 1984
Welsh Professional: 1985, 1986, 1988
Camus Hong Kong Masters: 1985
BCE Belgian Classic: 1986

World Ranking Positions

1979/80	8	1983/84	9	1987/88	6
1980/81	5	1984/85	8	1988/89	5
1981/82	3	1985/86	8	1989/90	5
1982/83	14	1986/87	10	1990/91	6

MIKE HALLETT

World ranking: Number 7
Date of birth: 6 July 1959
Star sign: Cancer

Prize money 1989/90: £113,877.38
Turned professional: 1979
Country: England

Mike Hallett dropped one place to number 7 in the world rankings after a disappointing finale to the season when he lost 13–8 to Darren Morgan in the second round of the World Championship. Hallett had been publicly criticised by his manager, Ian Doyle, for 'too much wining and dining' – a criticism that Mike accepted. In the end Hallett was grateful to stay in the top eight when, in fact, he had been looking for a move into the top four. The season had started so well for him when he came from 8–6 down to beat Dene O'Kane 9–8 in the final of the Hong Kong Open – Hallett's first ranking tournament success of his career.

The champ: Mike Hallett won his first ranking tournament title in the Hong Kong Open.

BEST PERFORMANCES

Embassy World Championship:
Quarter-finalist 1987 (lost to Neal Foulds 13–9)
Quarter-finalist 1989 (lost to Steve Davis 13–3)

Other Ranking Tournaments
Hong Kong Open:
Winner 1989 (beat Dene O'Kane 9–8)
555 Asian Open:
Round 4 1989 (lost to James Wattana 5–3)
BCE International:
Semi-finalist 1987 (lost to Steve Davis 9–3)
Rothmans Grand Prix:
Round 3 (last 16) 1983 (lost to Tony Meo 5–3)
Round 3 (last 16) 1984 (lost to Kirk Stevens 5–3)
Round 5 1986 (lost to Jimmy White 5–3)
Round 5 1988 (lost to Dennis Taylor 5–2)
Dubai Duty Free Classic:
Round 3 1989 (lost to Tony Jones 5–4)
StormSeal UK Open:
Quarter-finalist 1987 (lost to Joe Johnson 9–7)
Quarter-finalist 1989 (lost to Steve Davis 9–5)
Mercantile Credit Classic:
Round 1 (last 16) 1984 (lost to Tony Knowles 5–3)
Pearl Assurance British Open:
Runner-up 1988 (lost to Stephen Hendry 13–2)
European Open:
Semi-finalist 1989 (lost to John Parrott 5–4)

Current Non-ranking Tournaments
Benson and Hedges Masters:
Runner-up 1988 (lost to Steve Davis 9–0)
Benson and Hedges Irish Masters:
Quarter-finalist 1989 (lost to Steve Davis 5–4)
Everest World Matchplay:
Quarter-finalist 1988 (lost to Steve Davis 9–2)
Regal Masters:
Quarter-finalist 1989 (lost to Stephen Hendry 6–1)

Other Wins
British Isles Under-16: 1975
Foster's World Doubles: 1987
Foster's Professional: 1988
English Professional: 1989

World Ranking Positions

1980/81	–	1984/85	25	1987/88	16
1981/82	29	1985/86	28	1988/89	9
1982/83	31	1986/87	27	1989/90	6
1983/84	32			1990/91	7

DEAN REYNOLDS

World ranking: Number 8
Date of birth: 11 January 1963
Star sign: Capricorn

Prize money 1989/90: £100,915.25
Turned professional: 1981
Country: England

Chart success: Grimsby's Dean Reynolds is a solid left-hander who is looking to climb higher after jumping into the top ten at number 8. He is a former English champion looking for his first success in a ranking event.

Dean Reynolds, the left-hander from Grimsby, jumped seven places up the rankings to number 8 after a consistent season that saw him reach the final of the Rothmans Grand Prix. Unfortunately, he lost that final 10–0 to Steve Davis, but then gained his revenge when he beat Davis 9–7 in the quarter-finals of the Everest World Matchplay. Reynolds reached the second round of the World Championship but went out 13–11 to John Parrott after a long intense battle.

BEST PERFORMANCES

Embassy World Championship:
Quarter-finalist 1989 (lost to Tony Meo 13–9)

Other Ranking Tournaments
Hong Kong Open:
Round 3 1989 (lost to Jim Chambers 5–4)
555 Asian Open:
Round 4 1989 (lost to Wayne Jones 5–2)
BCE International:
Semi-finalist 1988 (lost to Jimmy White 9–5)
Rothmans Grand Prix:
Runner-up 1989 (lost to Steve Davis 10–0)
Dubai Duty Free Classic:
Quarter-finalist 1989 (lost to Stephen Hendry 5–3)
StormSeal UK Open:
Round 5 1986 (lost to Steve Davis 9–5)
Round 5 1988 (lost to Terry Griffiths 9–6)
Round 5 1989 (lost to Stephen Hendry 9–8)
Mercantile Credit Classic:
Semi-finalist 1987 (lost to Jimmy White 9–8)
Pearl Assurance British Open:
Runner-up 1989 (lost to Tony Meo 13–6)
European Open:
Round 4 1990 (lost to Nigel Bond 5–4)

Current Non-ranking Tournaments
Benson and Hedges Masters:
Round 1 1983 (lost to Ray Reardon 5–1)
Round 1 1988 (lost to Steve Davis 5–2)
Everest World Matchplay:
Semi-finalist 1989 (lost to Jimmy White 9–8)

Other Wins
British Isles Under-19: 1981
Junior Pot Black: 1981
English Professional: 1988

World Ranking Positions

1982/83	22	1985/86	24	1988/89	22
1983/84	19	1986/87	29	1989/90	15
1984/85	22	1987/88	15	1990/91	8

STEVE JAMES

World ranking: Number 9
Date of birth: 2 May 1961
Star sign: Taurus

Prize money 1989/90: £134,031.25
Turned professional: 1986
Country: England

Steve James enjoyed a remarkable second half to the season when he won the Mercantile Credit Classic and went on to reach the semi-finals of the Pearl Assurance British Open and the European Open in the space of just nine weeks. The fourteen points he gained from those three tournaments lifted him to number 9 in the rankings though he failed to get past the second round of the World Championship, losing 13–7 to Steve Davis. But while there was triumph James was also diagnosed as being a diabetic, which meant he had to make dramatic changes in his lifestyle with regard to eating and drinking. Away from the circuit, James is a committed motor-cycle fan and rides bikes that are capable of speeds up to 170 mph.

On the march: Steve James, the Mercantile Credit Classic champion, can still smile despite his defeat in the Benson and Hedges Masters.

BEST PERFORMANCES

Embassy World Championship:
Quarter-finalist 1988 (lost to Cliff Thorburn 13–11)

Other Ranking Tournaments
Hong Kong Open:
Round 4 1989 (lost to Ian Graham 5–3)
555 Asian Open:
Round 4 1989 (lost to Steve Duggan 5–3)
BCE International:
Semi-finalist 1988 (lost to Steve Davis 9–1)
Rothmans Grand Prix:
Round 4 1988 (lost to Mike Hallett 5–2)
Dubai Duty Free Classic:
Round 5 1989 (lost to John Parrott 5–3)

StormSeal UK Open:
Round 4 1988 (lost to Cliff Thorburn 9–6)
Mercantile Credit Classic:
Winner 1990 (beat Warren King 10–6)
Pearl Assurance British Open:
Semi-finalist 1990 (lost to Alex Higgins 9–3)
European Open:
Semi-finalist 1990 (lost to John Parrott 6–3)

Other Wins
No significant wins

World Ranking Positions

1987/88	67	1988/89	32	1990/91	9
		1989/90	16		

DENNIS TAYLOR

World ranking: Number 10
Date of birth: 19 January 1949
Star sign: Capricorn

Prize money 1989/90: £114,645.83
Turned professional: 1971
Country: Northern Ireland

Dennis Taylor's best performance came in the Benson and Hedges Irish Masters when, against a backdrop of controversy, he reached the final only to lose 9–4 to Steve Davis. Taylor arrived in Ireland after a bitter verbal row with Alex Higgins in the British Car Rental World Cup final, an incident for which Taylor reported Higgins for remarks that he made. Taylor and Higgins met in the quarter-finals of the Irish Masters and there was intense media pressure before, during and after the match which Taylor won 5–2. In the ranking tournaments Taylor reached just two quarter-finals – the Hong Kong Open and the Rothmans Grand Prix – but will be hoping this season to move back into the top eight after a change in management. After five years with Barry Hearn's Matchroom organisation, Taylor has teamed up with Foremost, a sports management company whose chairman is golfer Tony Jacklin. The highlight of Taylor's career came in 1985 when he won the world title.

BEST PERFORMANCES

Embassy World Championship:
Winner 1985 (beat Steve Davis 18–17)

Other Ranking Tournaments
Hong Kong Open:
Quarter-finalist 1989 (lost to Gary Wilkinson 5–3)
555 Asian Open:
Round 3 1989 (lost to Dave Gilbert 5–1)
BCE International:
Semi-finalist 1985 (lost to Cliff Thorburn 9–5)
Rothmans Grand Prix:
Winner 1984 (beat Cliff Thorburn 10–2)
Dubai Duty Free Classic:
Did not enter
StormSeal UK Open:
Semi-finalist 1985 (lost to Willie Thorne 9–7)
Mercantile Credit Classic:
Quarter-finalist 1988 (lost to John Parrott 5–1)
Pearl Assurance British Open:
Quarter-finalist 1985 (lost to Kirk Stevens 5–2)
Quarter-finalist 1987 (lost to Tony Knowles 5–4)
European Open:
Round 4 1989 (lost to Doug Mountjoy 5–3)

Current Non-ranking Tournaments
Benson and Hedges Masters:
Winner 1987 (beat Alex Higgins 9–8)
Benson and Hedges Irish Masters:
Runner-up 1990 (lost to Steve Davis 9–4)
Everest World Matchplay:
Quarter-finalist 1988 (Stephen Hendry 9–7)
Quarter-finalist 1989 (lost to John Parrott 9–6)
Regal Masters:
Round 1 1989 (lost to John Rea 6–5)

Other Wins
Irish Professional: 1982, 1985, 1986, 1987
Costa del Sol Classic: 1984
Guinness World Cup: 1985
BCE Canadian Masters: 1985
Camus Thailand Masters: 1985
Kit-Kat Break for World Champions: 1985
Winfield Masters: 1986
Car Care Plan World Cup: 1986
Tuborg World Cup: 1987
Carling Challenge: 1987
Labatt Canadian Masters: 1987
Matchroom Trophy: 1987
British Caledonian Tokyo Masters: 1987

World Ranking Positions

1976/77	9	1984/85	11
1977/78	4	1985/86	4
1978/79	8	1986/87	3
1979/80	2	1987/88	8
1980/81	6	1988/89	10
1981/82	5	1989/90	8
1982/83	13	1990/91	10
1983/84	13		

Swinging along: Dennis Taylor, a golfing fanatic, stayed in the top ten at number 10.

WILLIE THORNE

World ranking: Number 11
Date of birth: 4 March 1954
Star sign: Pisces

Prize money 1989/90: £111,456.46
Turned professional: 1975
Country: England

Willie Thorne is fully aware that his undoubted talent should have reaped many more rewards during his career. He has only one major title to his name in this country – the Mercantile Credit Classic in 1985 – but even so on his day he remains one of the most talented performers in the game. Thorne won the Lion Brown Masters in New Zealand at the start of the season while his best performance in a ranking event came in the 555 Asian Open where he lost 5–2 to Stephen Hendry in the last eight. In the World Championship, he reached the second round but, after holding an 11–8 lead, went out 13–11 to Neal Foulds. Thorne has left the Matchroom stable and joined Cue Tech.

BEST PERFORMANCES

Embassy World Championship:
Quarter-finalist 1982 (lost to Alex Higgins 13–10)
Quarter-finalist 1986 (lost to Cliff Thorburn 13–6)

Other Ranking Tournaments
Hong Kong Open:
Round 5 1989 (lost to Neal Foulds 5–1)
555 Asian Open:
Quarter-finalist 1989 (lost to Stephen Hendry 5–2)
BCE International:
Quarter-finalist 1983 (lost to Eddie Charlton 5–0)
Quarter-finalist 1984 (lost to Eugene Hughes 5–2)
Rothmans Grand Prix:
Semi-finalist 1983 (lost to Tony Knowles 9–7)
Dubai Duty Free Classic:
Did not enter
StormSeal UK Open:
Runner-up 1985 (lost to Steve Davis 16–14)
Mercantile Credit Classic:
Winner 1985 (beat Cliff Thorburn 13–8)
Pearl Assurance British Open:
Runner-up 1986 (lost to Steve Davis 12–7)
European Open:
Round 5 1989 (lost to Jimmy White 5–3)

Current Non-ranking Tournaments
Benson and Hedges Masters:
Quarter-finalist 1986 (lost to Steve Davis 5–4)
Quarter-finalist 1987 (lost to Cliff Thorburn 5–3)
Quarter-finalist 1990 (lost to Stephen Hendry 5–1)
Benson and Hedges Irish Masters:
Runner-up 1986 (lost to Jimmy White 9–5)
Runner-up 1987 (lost to Steve Davis 9–1)
Everest World Matchplay:
Round 1 1988 (lost to Mike Hallett 9–8)
Round 1 1989 (lost to Doug Mountjoy 9–2)

Other Wins
British Isles Under-16: 1970
British Isles Under-19: 1973
Pontin's Open: 1980
Pontin's Professional: 1984
Camus Hong Kong Masters: 1986
Matchroom Trophy: 1986
Kent China Cup: 1987
Lion Brown Masters: 1989

World Ranking Positions

1976/77	–	1981/82	22	1986/87	7
1977/78	20	1982/83	16	1987/88	11
1978/79	15	1983/84	18	1988/89	13
1979/80	17	1984/85	12	1989/90	9
1980/81	19	1985/86	11	1990/91	11

Seeing double: Willie Thorne who won the New Zealand Masters but later slipped two places to number 11.

MARTIN CLARK

World ranking: Number 12
Date of birth: 27 October 1968
Star sign: Scorpio

Prize money 1989/90: £48,453.12
Turned professional: 1987
Country: England

Martin Clark continued his climb up the rankings and is now guaranteed a place in the top sixteen for the first time at number 12. Two years ago he was a surprise casualty in the final qualifying round of the World Championship and he went out again at the same stage last season when he was beaten 10–9 by Welshman Tony Chappel. Clark, however, looks certain of a glittering career and scored points in all the major ranking tournaments – apart from the World Championship.

Young star: Martin Clark after receiving his Young Player of the Year award at the annual WPBSA dinner at the Hilton Hotel in London.

BEST PERFORMANCES

Embassy World Championship:
Qualifying round 5 1989 (lost to Bob Chaperon 10–4)
Qualifying round 5 1990 (lost to Tony Chappel 10–9)

Other Ranking Tournaments
Hong Kong Open:
Round 5 1989 (lost to Dennis Taylor 5–3)
555 Asian Open:
Quarter-finalist 1989 (lost to Gary Wilkinson 5–0)
BCE International:
Round 5 1987 (lost to Joe O'Boye 5–2)
Rothmans Grand Prix:
Round 4 1987 (lost to Mick Fisher 5–4)
Round 4 1989 (lost to Tony Knowles 5–2)
Dubai Duty Free Classic:
Round 5 1989 (lost to Danny Fowler 5–3)
StormSeal UK Open:
Round 4 1988 (lost to Danny Fowler 9–6)
Round 4 1989 (lost to Joe Johnson 9–6)
Mercantile Credit Classic:
Quarter-finalist 1989 (lost to Willie Thorne 5–4)
Pearl Assurance British Open:
Quarter-finalist 1989 (lost to Mike Hallett 5–3)
Quarter-finalist 1990 (lost to Alex Higgins 5–3)
European Open:
Quarter-finalist 1989 (lost to Terry Griffiths 5–1)

Other Wins
British Isles Under-19: 1984

World Ranking Positions

| 1988/89 41 | 1989/90 17 | 1990/91 12 |

NEAL FOULDS

World ranking: Number 13
Date of birth: 13 July 1963
Star sign: Cancer

Prize money 1989/90: £70,328.12
Turned professional: 1983
Country: England

Neal Foulds, after two seasons in the doldrums, eventually repeated the form that took him to world number 3 as he came through to the quarter-final of the Embassy World Championship. That performance, coupled with two quarter-final places from the previous two tournaments, lifted him back into the top sixteen. Foulds now has the platform to regain his place in the top ten this season and certainly he is one of the most popular players on the circuit. His finest moment came in 1986 when he won the BCE International and he was also a member of England's World Cup-winning team in 1988 and 1989.

Back in business: A determined Neal Foulds has returned to the top sixteen at number 13.

BEST PERFORMANCES

Embassy World Championship:
Semi-finalist 1987 (lost to Joe Johnson 16–9)

Other Ranking Tournaments
Hong Kong Open:
Quarter-finalist 1989 (lost to Jimmy White 5–2)
555 Asian Open:
Round 4 1989 (lost to Tony Knowles 5–3)
BCE International:
Winner 1986 (beat Cliff Thorburn 12–9)
Rothmans Grand Prix:
Semi-finalist 1984 (lost to Dennis Taylor 9–3)
Semi-finalist 1986 (lost to Rex Williams 9–8)
Dubai Duty Free Classic:
Did not enter
StormSeal UK Open:
Runner-up 1986 (lost to Steve Davis 16–7)
Mercantile Credit Classic:
Quarter-finalist 1986 (lost to Doug Mountjoy 5–3)
Pearl Assurance British Open:
Runner-up 1987 (lost to Jimmy White 13–9)
European Open:
Quarter-finalist 1990 (lost to Stephen Hendry 5–3)

Current Non-ranking Tournaments
Benson and Hedges Masters:
Semi-finalist 1989 (lost to John Parrott 6–5)
Benson and Hedges Irish Masters:
Runner-up 1988 (lost to Steve Davis 9–4)

Other Wins
British Isles Under-19: 1982
Pontin's Open: 1984
Pontin's Professional: 1987
Fersina Windows World Cup: 1988, 1989
Dubai Duty Free Masters: 1988

World Ranking Positions

1984/85 30	1986/87 13	1989/90 20
1985/86 23	1987/88 3	1990/91 13
	1988/89 3	

JOHN VIRGO

World ranking: Number 14
Date of birth: 4 March 1946
Star sign: Pisces

Prize money 1989/90: £44,405.62
Turned professional: 1976
Country: England

John Virgo hung on to his place in snooker's top sixteen after a traumatic season in which he was deposed as chairman of the WPBSA. He had a consistent 1989/90 season without reaching a major quarter-final. In the Embassy World Championship, he scored a 10–6 first-round victory over Gary Wilkinson, but then went out 13–6 to Jimmy White in the last sixteen. Virgo has always been a popular performer at exhibition nights and is well known for his impersonations of the game's top stars.

Tough time: John Virgo moved to number 14 after a season in which he was deposed as WPBSA chairman.

BEST PERFORMANCES

Embassy World Championship:
Semi-finalist 1979 (lost to Dennis Taylor 19–12)

Other Ranking Tournaments
Hong Kong Open:
Round 5 1989 (lost to Mike Hallett 5–1)
555 Asian Open:
Round 5 1989 (lost to Willie Thorne 5–2)
BCE International:
Semi-finalist 1982 (lost to David Taylor 9–5)
Rothmans Grand Prix:
Semi-finalist 1982 (lost to Jimmy White 10–4)
Dubai Duty Free Classic:
Round 5 1989 (lost to Jack McLaughlin 5–4)
StormSeal UK Open:
Quarter-finalist 1988 (lost to Doug Mountjoy 9–8)
Mercantile Credit Classic:
Quarter-finalist 1985 (lost to Willie Thorne 5–1)
Pearl Assurance British Open:
Semi-finalist 1986 (lost to Willie Thorne 9–4)
European Open:
Round 5 1989 (lost to Eddie Charlton 5–4)

Current Non-ranking Tournaments
Benson and Hedges Masters:
Round 1 1980 (lost to Cliff Thorburn 5–3)
Round 1 1983 (lost to Doug Mountjoy 5–1)
Round 1 1984 (lost to Ray Reardon 5–3)
Round 1 1989 (lost to Jimmy White 5–2)
Round 1 1990 (lost to Jimmy White 5–3)

Other Wins
British Isles Under-16: 1962
British Isles Under-19: 1965
Coral UK: 1979
Pontin's Professional: 1980
Bombay International: 1980
Professional Snooker League: 1984

World Ranking Positions

1977/78	18	1984/85	18
1978/79	19	1985/86	19
1979/80	10	1986/87	19
1980/81	12	1987/88	19
1981/82	13	1988/89	15
1982/83	19	1989/90	13
1983/84	14	1990/91	14

WHO SAID THAT?

'I'm not bitter, but I am very pleased to be out of it. It got to the stage where I didn't know if I was going to a tournament as a player or an official.'

▲

– John Virgo talking about his time as chairman of the WPBSA.

TONY MEO

World ranking: Number 15
Date of birth: 4 October 1959
Star sign: Libra

Prize money 1989/90: £82,555.87
Turned professional: 1979
Country: England

Tony Meo managed to stay in the top sixteen at number 15 after a series of indifferent performances. Yet, in the previous season, he had captured the British Open title and reached the semi-final of the World Championship. In 1989/90, however, his best display came in the World Championship where he reached the last sixteen before losing to Stephen Hendry. After taking seventeen points in the 1988/89 season, Meo had to settle for seven points in 1989/90 and will be hoping for improved performances during this campaign.

BEST PERFORMANCES
Embassy World Championship:
Semi-final 1989 (lost to John Parrott 16–7)

Other Ranking Tournaments
Hong Kong Open:
Round 4 1989 (lost to Alex Higgins 5–4)
555 Asian Open:
Round 4 1989 (lost to Gary Wilkinson 5–2)
BCE International:
Quarter-finalist 1988 (lost to Steve James 5–1)
Rothmans Grand Prix:
Semi-finalist 1983 (lost to Joe Johnson 9–6)
Dubai Duty Free Classic:
Did not enter
StormSeal UK Open:
Round 2 (last 16) 1984 (lost to Steve Davis 9–7)
Round 5 1985 (lost to Steve Davis 9–5)
Mercantile Credit Classic:
Runner-up 1984 (lost to Steve Davis 9–8)
Pearl Assurance British Open:
Winner 1989 (beat Dean Reynolds 13–6)
European Open:
Round 3 1989 (lost to David Roe 5–1)
Round 3 1990 (lost to Craig Edwards 5–4)

Current Non-ranking Tournaments
Benson and Hedges Masters:
Semi-finalist 1982 (lost to Steve Davis 6–4)
Semi-finalist 1987 (lost to Alex Higgins 6–2)
Benson and Hedges Irish Masters:
Quarter-finalist 1982 (lost to Terry Griffiths 5–3)
Quarter-finalist 1983 (lost to Ray Reardon 5–4)
Quarter-finalist 1984 (lost to Steve Davis 5–4)
Quarter-finalist 1986 (lost to Jimmy White 5–2)
Quarter-finalist 1987 (lost to Steve Davis 5–2)

Other Wins
British Isles Under-19: 1978
Winfield Masters: 1981, 1985
Hofmeister World Doubles: 1982, 1983, 1985, 1986
State Express World Team Classic: 1983
English Professional: 1986, 1987
Matchroom International League: 1990

World Ranking Positions

1980/81	–	1986/87	11
1981/82	18	1987/88	20
1982/83	24	1988/89	31
1983/84	15	1989/90	14
1984/85	10	1990/91	15
1985/86	10		

Disappointment: Tony Meo did not enjoy a good season on the ranking circuit but he did win the Matchroom International League.

ALAIN ROBIDOUX

World ranking: Number 16
Date of birth: 25 July 1960
Star sign: Leo

Prize money 1989/90: £65,375.00
Turned professional: 1986 (earned full status 1988)
Country: Canada

Alain Robidoux enjoyed the best season of his career and climaxed a spectacular rise up the ranks by moving into the top sixteen for the first time. He was originally ranked number 17 but moved up one place after Alex Higgins was banned for a season and penalised 25 ranking points. In Robidoux's first-round match in the Embassy World Championship against Stephen Hendry, the Canadian claimed that a controversial 'push shot' decision cost him the match as he went down 10–7. He reached the semi-final of the BCE International before losing 6–3 to Steve Davis, while the highlight of his season was helping Canada win the British Car Rental World Cup – a tournament in which he played a starring role, winning ten of his twelve frames.

French connection: Alain Robidoux, the French Canadian, who gained a place in the top sixteen for the first time at number 16.

BEST PERFORMANCES

Embassy World Championship:
Round 1 1990 (lost to Stephen Hendry 10–7)

Other Ranking Tournaments
Hong Kong Open:
Round 4 1989 (lost to Stephen Hendry 5–4)
555 Asian Open:
Round 2 1989 (lost to Steve Campbell 5–2)
BCE International:
Semi-finalist 1989 (lost to Steve Davis 6–3)
Rothmans Grand Prix:
Semi-finalist 1988 (lost to Alex Higgins 9–7)
Dubai Duty Free Classic:
Round 4 1989 (lost to Nigel Bond 5–4)
StormSeal UK Open:
Quarter-finalist 1989 (lost to Terry Griffiths 9–2)

Mercantile Credit Classic:
Round 2 1989 (lost to Bill Werbeniuk 5–4)
Round 2 1990 (lost to Andrew Cairns 5–4)
Pearl Assurance British Open:
Round 5 1990 (lost to Bob Chaperon 5–4)
European Open:
Round 5 1989 (lost to Terry Griffiths 5–3)

Other Wins
Canadian Amateur: 1983, 1985, 1987
Canadian Professional: 1988
British Car Rental World Cup: 1990

World Ranking Positions

1988/89	102	1989/90	35	1990/91	16

JOE JOHNSON

World ranking: Number 17
Date of birth: 29 July 1952
Star sign: Leo

Prize money 1989/90: £84,061.28
Turned professional: 1979
Country: England

Going down: Joe Johnson, the 1986 world champion, dropped down to number 17 from number 11.

Joe Johnson, after six seasons in the top sixteen, dropped to number 17. It has been a gradual decline for the popular Yorkshireman who captivated television audiences when he beat Steve Davis 18–12 to win the Embassy World Championship in 1986. But last season Johnson failed to progress past the first round of the World Championship, when he was beaten 10–8 by the rapidly improving Darren Morgan. However, he did win the Norwich Union Grand Prix.

BEST PERFORMANCES

Embassy World Championship:
Winner 1986 (beat Steve Davis 18–12)

Other Ranking Tournaments
Hong Kong Open:
Round 3 1989 (lost to Les Dodd 5–0)
555 Asian Open:
Round 4 1989 (lost to Tony Drago 5–2)
BCE International:
Quarter-finalist 1985 (lost to Neal Foulds 5–2)
Quarter-finalist 1988 (lost to Dean Reynolds 5–1)
Rothmans Grand Prix:
Runner-up 1983 (lost to Tony Knowles 9–8)
Dubai Duty Free Classic:
Round 3 1989 (lost to Nigel Bond 5–3)
StormSeal UK Open:
Semi-finalist 1987 (lost to Jimmy White 9–4)
Mercantile Credit Classic:
Semi-finalist 1985 (lost to Cliff Thorburn 9–2)
Pearl Assurance British Open:
Quarter-finalist 1989 (lost to Dean Reynolds 5–4)
European Open:
Round 5 1989 (lost to Martin Clark 5–4)
Round 5 1990 (lost to John Parrott 5–2)

Current Non-ranking Tournaments
Benson and Hedges Masters:
Semi-finalist 1988 (lost to Steve Davis 6–3)
Benson and Hedges Irish Masters:
Quarter-finalist 1987 (lost to Terry Griffiths 5–0)
Quarter-finalist 1988 (lost to Steve Davis 5–0)
Everest World Matchplay:
Quarter-finalist 1988 (lost to John Parrott 9–7)

Other Wins
British Isles Under-19: 1971
Langs Supreme Masters: 1987
Norwich Union Grand Prix: 1989

World Ranking Positions

1980/81	–	1986/87	8
1981/82	–	1987/88	5
1982/83	–	1988/89	11
1983/84	23	1989/90	11
1984/85	19	1990/91	17
1985/86	16		

CLIFF THORBURN

World ranking: Number 18
Date of birth: 16 January 1948
Star sign: Capricorn

Prize money 1989/90: £80,234.34
Turned professional: 1973
Country: Canada

Canadian Cliff Thorburn endured a season he would rather forget and slipped out of the top sixteen for the first time in his career. He won just four matches before going to the Embassy World Championship, but then recovered some of the lost ground by reaching the quarter-final which he then lost 13–6 to John Parrott. Even so, those four points were not enough to save his top-sixteen place. Thorburn is still the only overseas player to have won the World Championship and is also in the record books as the only professional to have scored two competitive 147 breaks. The first maximum came at the World Championship in 1983 and the second during a Matchroom League match in Sussex in 1989. Thorburn also skippered Canada to their second victory in the British Car Rental World Cup last season.

The thinker: Canadian Cliff Thorburn who suffered a slide of eleven places to number 18.

BEST PERFORMANCES

Embassy World Championship:
Winner 1980 (beat Alex Higgins 18–16)

Other Ranking Tournaments
Hong Kong Open:
Round 3 1989 (lost to Tony Jones 5–2)
555 Asian Open:
Round 3 1989 (lost to Tony Jones 5–2)
BCE International:
Winner 1985 (beat Jimmy White 12–10)
Rothmans Grand Prix:
Runner-up 1984 (lost to Dennis Taylor 10–2)
Dubai Duty Free Classic:
Did not enter
StormSeal UK Open:
Semi-finalist 1984 (lost to Alex Higgins 9–7)
Mercantile Credit Classic:
Runner-up 1985 (lost to Willie Thorne 13–8)
Runner-up 1986 (lost to Jimmy White 13–12)
Pearl Assurance British Open:
Semi-finalist 1987 (lost to Jimmy White 9–5)
Semi-finalist 1988 (lost to Stephen Hendry 9–5)
European Open:
Quarter-finalist 1989 (lost to Jimmy White 5–3)

Current Non-ranking Tournaments
Benson and Hedges Masters:
Winner 1983 (beat Ray Reardon 9–7)
Winner 1985 (beat Doug Mountjoy 9–6)
Winner 1986 (beat Jimmy White 9–5)
Benson and Hedges Irish Masters:
Semi-finalist 1981 (lost to Terry Griffiths 6–5)
Semi-finalist 1986 (lost to Willie Thorne 6–4)
Everest World Matchplay:
Round 1 1988 (lost to Joe Johnson 9–4)
Round 1 1989 (lost to Terry Griffiths 9–5)

Other Wins
Canadian Open: 1974, 1978, 1979, 1980
Pot Black: 1981
Winfield Masters: 1983
Canadian Professional: 1984, 1985, 1986, 1987
Langs Supreme Masters: 1985, 1986
British Car Rental World Cup: 1982, 1990

World Ranking Positions

1976/77 3	1981/82 1	1986/87 2
1977/78 6	1982/83 3	1987/88 4
1978/79 5	1983/84 3	1988/89 6
1979/80 5	1984/85 3	1989/90 7
1980/81 2	1985/86 2	1990/91 18

GARY WILKINSON

World ranking: Number 19
Date of birth: 7 April 1966
Star sign: Aries

Prize money 1989/90: £65,030.62
Turned professional: 1987
Country: England

Signing on: Gary Wilkinson, the world number 19, as he signs a management contract with Cuemasters chairman Ian Doyle.

Gary Wilkinson looked a certainty for the top sixteen when he reached three semi-finals in the first half of the season – the Hong Kong Open, the Dubai Duty Free Classic and the StormSeal UK Open. In the UK Open he seemed sure to beat Steve Davis in the semi-final, but then embarrassingly miscounted at a vital moment and lost the match 9–8. Sadly, Wilkinson didn't fulfil that early promise in the remainder of the season, though he did make a major career decision when he joined Ian Doyle's Cuemasters squad. He moved up twenty places from number 39, but deep down he knows he should have been even higher.

BEST PERFORMANCES

Embassy World Championship:
Round 1 1989 (lost to Stephen Hendry 10–9)
Round 1 1990 (lost to John Virgo 10–6)

Other Ranking Tournaments
Hong Kong Open:
Semi-finalist 1989 (lost to Dene O'Kane 5–3)
555 Asian Open:
Semi-finalist 1989 (lost to Stephen Hendry 5–4)
BCE International:
Round 3 1987 (lost to Stephen Hendry 5–4)
Rothmans Grand Prix:
Round 5 1987 (lost to Steve Newbury 5–3)
Dubai Duty Free Classic:
Round 4 1989 (lost to Joe Grech 5–2)

StormSeal UK Open:
Semi-finalist 1989 (lost to Steve Davis 9–8)
Mercantile Credit Classic:
Round 5 1990 (lost to Wayne Jones 5–2)
Pearl Assurance British Open:
Round 5 1988 (lost to Jimmy White 5–1)
European Open:
Round 4 1989 (lost to John Parrott 5–2)

Other Wins
No significant wins

World Ranking Positions

1987/88 –	1988/89 45	1990/91 19
	1989/90 39	

STEVE NEWBURY

World ranking: Number 20
Date of birth: 21 April 1956
Star sign: Taurus

Prize money 1989/90: £44,000.00
Turned professional: 1984
Country: Wales

Welshman Steve Newbury will be one of the favourites to clinch a top-sixteen place by the end of this season after gaining fourteen points during 1989/90. His consistency saw him reach the quarter-finals of the Mercantile Credit Classic and the Pearl Assurance British Open. In the British Open, Newbury produced arguably the best performance of his career when he beat Steve Davis 5–2 in the fifth round before going out 5–4 to Robert Marshall in the quarter-finals. Newbury, from Neath, was a busy man last season as he redecorated his new house, but he still found time for plenty of practice. In the World Championship he was beaten 10–9 by Mike Hallett in round 1.

Aiming higher: Welshman Steve Newbury will this season be looking for a place in the top sixteen.

BEST PERFORMANCES

Embassy World Championship:
Round 1 1989 (lost to Steve Davis 10–5)
Round 1 1990 (lost to Mike Hallett 10–9)

Other Ranking Tournaments
Hong Kong Open:
Round 5 1989 (lost to Gary Wilkinson 5–1)
555 Asian Open:
Round 3 1989 (lost to Steve Duggan 5–3)
BCE International:
Round 2 (last 16) 1984 (lost to Tony Knowles 5–4)
Round 5 1988 (lost to Joe Johnson 5–2)
Round 5 1989 (lost to Alain Robidoux 5–2)
Rothmans Grand Prix:
Quarter-finalist 1987 (lost to Dennis Taylor 5–2)
Dubai Duty Free Classic:
Round 3 1985 (lost to John Campbell 5–1)

StormSeal UK Open:
Round 3 1985 (lost to Kirk Stevens 9–7)
Round 3 1987 (lost to John Parrott 9–5)
Round 3 1988 (lost to Colin Roscoe 9–7)
Round 3 1989 (lost to Tony Jones 9–7)
Mercantile Credit Classic:
Semi-finalist 1988 (lost to Steve Davis 9–2)
Pearl Assurance British Open:
Quarter-finalist 1990 (lost to Robert Marshall 5–4)
European Open:
Round 4 1990 (lost to Stephen Hendry 5–1)

Other Wins
Welsh Amateur: 1980

World Ranking Positions

1985/86	34	1988/89	25
1986/87	40	1989/90	19
1987/88	45	1990/91	20

TONY KNOWLES

World ranking: Number 21
Date of birth: 13 June 1955
Star sign: Gemini

Prize money 1989/90: £63,687.50
Turned professional: 1980
Country: England

Tony Knowles dropped out of the world's top sixteen for the first time since 1982, but he is confident that it is only a minor setback in his long career. Knowles, who was world number 2 in 1984/85, reached only one quarter-final last season – in the Rothmans Grand Prix. A plain speaker, he has been highly critical of the sixteen table qualifying system at Blackpool, but accepts that he will have to cope with this pressure if he is to get back into snooker's elite top group. Knowles won his opening match in the World Championship, but then went out 13–6 to Terry Griffiths in the second round. In years gone by Knowles' personal life has often been the subject of newspaper headlines, but he now seems more settled and he has never been short of self-confidence. He lives in a luxury house in the Lake District.

Cheery chap: Tony Knowles still enjoys a laugh despite his absence from the top sixteen at number 21.

BEST PERFORMANCES

Embassy World Championship:
Semi-finalist 1983 (lost to Cliff Thorburn 16–15)
Semi-finalist 1985 (lost to Dennis Taylor 16–5)
Semi-finalist 1986 (lost to Joe Johnson 16–8)

Other Ranking Tournaments
Hong Kong Open:
Round 3 1989 (lost to Gary Wilkinson 5–2)
555 Asian Open:
Round 5 1989 (lost to Silvino Francisco 5–2)
BCE International:
Winner 1982 (beat David Taylor 9–6)
Rothmans Grand Prix:
Winner 1983 (beat Joe Johnson 9–8)
Dubai Duty Free Classic:
Round 3 1989 (lost to Joe Grech 5–3)
StormSeal UK Open:
Quarter-finalist 1984 (lost to Kirk Stevens 9–7)
Quarter-finalist 1985 (lost to Jimmy White 9–4)
Mercantile Credit Classic:
Semi-finalist 1988 (lost to John Parrott 9–4)
Pearl Assurance British Open:
Semi-finalist 1987 (lost to Neal Foulds 9–2)
European Open:
Round 3 1989 (lost to Danny Fowler 5–2)
Round 3 1990 (lost to Tony Chappel 5–3)

Current Non-ranking Tournaments
Benson and Hedges Masters:
Semi-finalist 1984 (lost to Terry Griffiths 6–4)
Semi-finalist 1986 (lost to Cliff Thorburn 6–4)
Benson and Hedges Irish Masters:
Semi-finalist 1985 (lost to Jimmy White 6–4)
Everest World Matchplay:
Round 1 1988 (lost to Dennis Taylor 9–7)

Other Wins
British Isles Under-19: 1972, 1974
Pontin's Autumn Open: 1979
State Express World Team Classic: 1983
Winfield Masters: 1984

World Ranking Positions

1981/82	20	1986/87	4
1982/83	15	1987/88	7
1983/84	4	1988/89	8
1984/85	2	1989/90	12
1985/86	3	1990/91	21

WAYNE JONES

World ranking: Number 22
Date of birth: 24 December 1959
Star sign: Capricorn

Prize money 1989/90: £36,983.75
Turned professional: 1984
Country: Wales

Wayne Jones is now established in the world's top thirty-two, and last season again found Blackpool his favourite tournament venue. In 1989 he reached the final of the Mercantile Credit Classic and last season came through to the last eight before losing 5–2 to Steve James. Jones' season was steady rather than spectacular, but he is now perfectly poised for a move into the top sixteen next season. There was disappointment in the World Championship when he was beaten 10–8 by Tony Meo in the first round. An intense family man, Welshman Jones is a quiet personality on the professional circuit and becomes homesick at overseas tournaments.

Steady climb: Wayne Jones rose nine places to number 22.

BEST PERFORMANCES

Embassy World Championship:
Round 2 1989 (lost to Dean Reynolds 13–9)

Other Ranking Tournaments
Hong Kong Open:
Round 4 1989 (lost to Willie Thorne 5–1)
555 Asian Open:
Round 5 1989 (lost Stephen Hendry 5–0)
BCE International:
Round 1 (last 32) 1984 (lost to David Taylor 5–4)
Round 4 1987 (lost to Nigel Gilbert 5–4)
Round 4 1989 (lost to Steve Davis 5–2)
Rothmans Grand Prix:
Round 4 1985 (lost to Peter Francisco 5–3)
Round 4 1986 (lost to Silvino Francisco 5–4)
Round 4 1988 (lost to Jimmy White 5–1)

Dubai Duty Free Classic:
Round 4 1989 (lost to Barry West 5–2)
StormSeal UK Open:
Quarter-finalist 1986 (lost to Alex Higgins 9–5)
Mercantile Credit Classic:
Runner-up 1989 (lost to Doug Mountjoy 13–11)
Pearl Assurance British Open:
Round 2 (last 32) 1985 (lost to Bob Chaperon 5–2)
European Open:
Round 4 1990 (lost to John Parrott 5–0)

Other Wins
British Isles Under-16: 1976
Welsh Amateur: 1983

World Ranking Positions

1985/86 49	1987/88 34	1989/90 31
1986/87 56	1988/89 34	1990/91 22

DENE O'KANE

World ranking: Number 23
Date of birth: 24 February 1963
Star sign: Pisces

Prize money 1989/90: £59,882.79
Turned professional: 1984
Country: New Zealand

Dene O'Kane, the highly talented New Zealander, has moved up the rankings to number 23, thanks to a brilliant performance in the Hong Kong Open, the opening ranking tournament of the season. He reached the final and looked like taking the £40,000 first prize when he led Mike Hallett 8–6. But O'Kane's title dream disappeared as Hallett took the final three frames for a 9–8 win. Even so, the five points he gained there plus a quarter-final place in the Mercantile Credit Classic gave him a solid base on which to build for this season. He was bitterly disappointed with his World Championship performance when he was crushed 10–2 by Canada's Alain Robidoux in the fifth qualifying round.

BEST PERFORMANCES

Embassy World Championship:
Quarter-finalist 1987 (lost to Jimmy White 13–6)

Other Ranking Tournaments
Hong Kong Open:
Runner-up 1989 (lost to Mike Hallett 9–8)
555 Asian Open:
Round 4 1989 (lost to John Virgo 5–3)
BCE International:
Round 1 (last 32) 1984 (lost to Willie Thorne 5–3)
Round 4 1986 (lost to Ken Owers 5–0)
Round 4 1988 (lost to Jim Wych 5–4)
Rothmans Grand Prix:
Round 4 1988 (lost to Alex Higgins 5–0)
Dubai Duty Free Classic:
Round 4 1989 (lost to Alex Higgins 5–3)
StormSeal UK Open:
Round 5 1987 (lost to Willie Thorne 9–7)
Mercantile Credit Classic:
Quarter-finalist 1990 (lost to Silvino Francisco 5–4)
Pearl Assurance British Open:
Quarter-finalist 1985 (lost to Steve Davis 5–1)
Quarter-finalist 1988 (lost to John Parrott 5–2)
European Open:
Round 4 1990 (lost to Craig Edwards 5–2)

Other Wins
New Zealand Amateur: 1980

World Ranking Positions

1985/86 32	1987/88 35	1989/90 28
1986/87 39	1988/89 24	1990/91 23

PETER FRANCISCO

World ranking: Number 24
Date of birth: 14 February 1962
Star sign: Aquarius

Prize money 1989/90: £34,681.25
Turned professional: 1984
Country: South Africa

South African Peter Francisco enjoyed a much better season as he reached the quarter-final of the Dubai Duty Free Classic and also picked up nine more ranking points to maintain his place in the top thirty-two. Francisco, who was number 14 in the 1988/89 season, is over his spell of injury and illness and will be hoping to continue his impressive run and move back towards the top sixteen. In the World Championship he went down 10–7 to Grimsby's Dean Reynolds in round 1.

BEST PERFORMANCES
Embassy World Championship:
Round 1 1988 (lost to Willie Thorne 10–6)
Round 1 1989 (lost to Dean Reynolds 10–7)
Round 1 1990 (lost to Dean Reynolds 10–7)

Other Ranking Tournaments
Hong Kong Open:
Round 3 1989 (lost to Alain Robidoux 5–3)
555 Asian Open:
Round 5 1989 (lost to Gary Wilkinson 5–4)
BCE International:
Semi-finalist 1986 (lost to Cliff Thorburn 9–7)
Rothmans Grand Prix:
Semi-finalist 1987 (lost to Dennis Taylor 9–4)
Dubai Duty Free Classic:
Quarter-finalist 1989 (lost to John Parrott 5–1)
StormSeal UK Open:
Round 5 1989 (lost to Mark Bennett 9–3)
Mercantile Credit Classic:
Round 5 1986 (lost to Steve Davis 5–0)
Round 5 1987 (lost to Silvino Francisco 5–1)
Round 5 1988 (lost to Dennis Taylor 5–3)
Round 5 1990 (lost to Steve Newbury 5–3)
Pearl Assurance British Open:
Quarter-finalist 1989 (lost to Tony Meo 5–3)
European Open:
Round 3 1989 (lost to John Campbell 5–0)
Round 3 1990 (lost to Colin Roscoe 5–3)

Current Non-ranking Tournaments
Benson and Hedges Masters:
Round 1 1989 (lost to Neal Foulds 5–2)
Everest World Matchplay:
Round 1 1988 (lost to Terry Griffiths 9–7)

Other Wins
South African Amateur: 1981, 1982, 1983

World Ranking Positions

1985/86	59	1988/89	14
1986/87	26	1989/90	25
1987/88	18	1990/91	24

In the driving seat: Peter Francisco was happy to stay in the top thirty-two at number 24.

BOB CHAPERON

World ranking: Number 25
Date of birth: 18 May 1958
Star sign: Taurus

Prize money 1989/90: £113,250.00
Turned professional: 1983
Country: Canada

What a season!: Bob Chaperon, pictured with the Pearl Assurance British Open trophy, also helped Canada to victory in the British Car Rental World Cup.

Bob Chaperon enjoyed the greatest season of his career in 1989/90, winning the Pearl Assurance British Open and helping Canada to success in the British Car Rental World Cup. Both those successes came in the same month, and he remarked: 'I will keep the diary page of March 1990 for the rest of my life.' Chaperon had been struggling for the early part of the season and his place in the top thirty-two looked in jeopardy, but then he produced a string of brilliant performances in the British Open at Derby and eventually beat Alex Higgins in the final to collect the £75,000 first prize. A couple of weeks later Chaperon, from Sudbury, Ontario, and his two Canadian colleagues, Alain Robidoux and Cliff Thorburn, went all the way to the World Cup final in Bournemouth where they beat Northern Ireland 9–5. Predictably, the celebrations continued long into the night. But Chaperon's fine run came to an end, and in the World Championship he failed to qualify after being beaten 10–9 by Welshman Darren Morgan.

BEST PERFORMANCES

Embassy World Championship:
Round 1 1988 (lost to Mike Hallett 10–2)
Round 1 1989 (lost to Terry Griffiths 10–6)

Other Ranking Tournaments
Hong Kong Open:
Round 4 1989 (lost to Martin Clark 5–2)
555 Asian Open:
Round 3 1989 (lost to Warren King 5–2)
BCE International:
Round 5 1986 (lost to Eugene Hughes 5–0)
Round 5 1988 (lost to Tony Meo 5–4)
Rothmans Grand Prix:
Quarter-finalist 1987 (lost to John Parrott 5–2)
Dubai Duty Free Classic:
Round 3 1989 (lost to Brian Rowswell 5–4)

StormSeal UK Open:
Round 4 1989 (lost to John Parrott 9–8)
Mercantile Credit Classic:
Round 4 1989 (lost to John Virgo 5–1)
Round 4 1990 (lost to Steve James 5–2)
Pearl Assurance British Open:
Winner 1990 (beat Alex Higgins 10–8)
European Open:
Round 4 1990 (lost to Steve Davis 5–0)

Other Wins
Canadian Amateur: 1981

World Ranking Positions

1984/85	–	1988/89	29
1985/86	44	1989/90	29
1986/87	53	1990/91	25
1987/88	41		

SILVINO FRANCISCO

World ranking: Number 26
Date of birth: 3 May 1946
Star sign: Taurus

Prize money 1989/90: £43,483.75
Turned professional: 1978
Country: South Africa

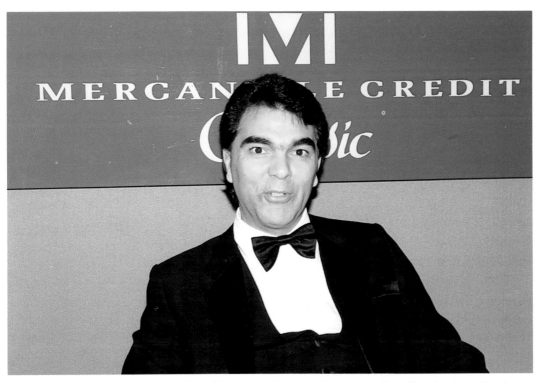

Happy man: Silvino Francisco was cleared by police of any involvement in alleged betting irregularities.

Silvino Francisco, once a regular member of snooker's top sixteen, maintained his place in the top thirty-two after a season that was surrounded by controversy. He was at the centre of police investigations into allegations of betting irregularities at the Benson and Hedges tournaments in 1986 and 1989, but the police decided that he was innocent of any involvement. He reached the semi-final of the Mercantile Credit Classic, and the gathering of six more points helped consolidate his position. In the World Championship Francisco was beaten 10–7 by Gary Wilkinson in the final qualifying round.

BEST PERFORMANCES

Embassy World Championship:
Quarter-finalist 1982 (lost to Ray Reardon 13–8)

Other Ranking Tournaments
Hong Kong Open:
Round 3 1989 (lost to Barry Pinches 5–4)
555 Asian Open:
Quarter-finalist 1989 (lost to James Wattana 5–2)
BCE International:
Semi-finalist 1984 (lost to Tony Knowles 9–6)
Rothmans Grand Prix:
Semi-finalist 1986 (lost to Jimmy White 9–6)
Dubai Duty Free Classic:
Round 3 1989 (lost to Paul Medati 5–4)
StormSeal UK Open:
Round 5 1985 (lost to Terry Griffiths 9–5)
Round 5 1987 (lost to Terry Griffiths 9–3)
Mercantile Credit Classic:
Semi-finalist 1990 (lost to Warren King 6–5)

Pearl Assurance British Open:
Winner 1985 (beat Kirk Stevens 12–9)
European Open:
Round 4 1990 (lost to Mark Bennett 5–3)

Current Non-ranking Tournaments
Benson and Hedges Masters:
Quarter-finalist 1987 (lost to Dennis Taylor 5–3)

Other Wins
South African Amateur: 1968, 1969, 1974, 1977
South African Professional: 1985, 1986

World Ranking Positions

1979/80	–	1985/86	13
1980/81	–	1986/87	12
1981/82	–	1987/88	10
1982/83	17	1988/89	12
1983/84	21	1989/90	23
1984/85	17	1990/91	26

BARRY WEST

World ranking: Number 27
Date of birth: 24 October 1958
Star sign: Scorpio

Prize money 1989/90: £24,796.25
Turned professional: 1985
Country: England

Barry West was last season hoping for a move into the top sixteen but he did not produce the form that saw him move up five places to number 21 the previous season. He reached the fifth round of ranking tournaments on three occasions but that's where the progress stopped, while he failed to qualify for the first round of the Embassy World Championship.

BEST PERFORMANCES

Embassy World Championship:
Round 1 1987 (lost to Ray Reardon 10–5)
Round 1 1988 (lost to Doug Mountjoy 10–6)

Other Ranking Tournaments
Hong Kong Open:
Round 4 1989 (lost to Mike Hallett 5–4)
555 Asian Open:
Round 5 1989 (lost to Martin Clark 5–0)
BCE International:
Quarter-finalist 1988 (lost to Jimmy White 5–2)
Rothmans Grand Prix:
Round 4 1988 (lost to Terry Griffiths 5–1)
Dubai Duty Free Classic:
Round 5 1989 (lost to Dean Reynolds 5–2)
StormSeal UK Open:
Quarter-finalist 1985 (lost to Steve Davis 9–1)
Quarter-finalist 1988 (lost to Terry Griffiths 9–5)
Mercantile Credit Classic:
Round 5 1987 (lost to Dean Reynolds 5–3)
Round 5 1988 (lost to Terry Griffiths 5–2)

Pearl Assurance British Open:
Round 5 1989 (lost to Peter Francisco 5–1)
European Open:
Round 3 1989 (lost to Murdo Macleod 5–4)
Round 3 1990 (lost to Danny Fowler 5–2)

Other Wins
No significant wins

World Ranking Positions

1986/87	30	1989/90	21
1987/88	29	1990/91	27
1988/89	26		

CLIFF WILSON

World ranking: Number 28
Date of birth: 10 May 1934
Star sign: Taurus

Prize money 1989/90: £29,258.75
Turned professional: 1979
Country: Wales

Cliff Wilson, a member of the world's top sixteen two seasons ago, is slipping down the rankings once again after an indifferent season that saw him reach just one quarter-final. That was in the BCE International when he went down 5–2 to Stephen Hendry. Wilson also continued his poor run at the World Championship when he was beaten 10–6 by Canadian Cliff Thorburn: he has never won a match at Sheffield's Crucible Theatre. Away from snooker, Wilson, a former world amateur champion, is a keen angler and was delighted with his trip to the Middle East for the Dubai Duty Free Classic when he managed to get out for a day's fishing.

BEST PERFORMANCES

Embassy World Championship:
Round 1 1980 (lost to Doug Mountjoy 10–6)
Round 1 1981 (lost to David Taylor 10–6)
Round 1 1982 (lost to Eddie Charlton 10–5)
Round 1 1983 (lost to Doug Mountjoy 10–2)

Round 1 1986 (lost to Eddie Charlton 10–6)
Round 1 1988 (lost to Joe Johnson 10–7)
Round 1 1989 (lost to Steve Duggan 10–1)
Round 1 1990 (lost to Cliff Thorburn 10–6)

Other Ranking Tournaments
Hong Kong Open:
Round 4 1989 (withdrew – illness)
555 Asian Open:
Round 3 1989 (lost to Brady Gollan 5–4)
BCE International:
Quarter-finalist 1982 (lost to Tony Knowles 5–4)
Quarter-finalist 1986 (lost to Cliff Thorburn 5–1)
Quarter-finalist 1989 (lost to Stephen Hendry 5–2)
Rothmans Grand Prix:
Quarter-finalist 1985 (lost to Dennis Taylor 5–2)
Dubai Duty Free Classic:
Round 4 1989 (lost to Tony Drago 5–0)
StormSeal UK Open:
Round 2 (last 16) 1984 (lost to Cliff Thorburn 9–3)
Mercantile Credit Classic:
Quarter-finalist 1987 (lost to Dean Reynolds 5–1)
Pearl Assurance British Open:
Round 5 1987 (lost to John Virgo 5–2)
Round 5 1989 (lost to Dean Reynolds 5–0)
European Open:
Round 4 1989 (lost to Alain Robidoux 5–0)

Current Non-ranking Tournaments
Benson and Hedges Masters:
Round 1 1989 (lost to Steve Davis 5–2)

Other Wins
British Isles Under-19: 1952, 1953
Welsh Amateur: 1956, 1977, 1979
World Amateur: 1978

World Ranking Positions

1980/81	–	1986/87	23
1981/82	23	1987/88	17
1982/83	26	1988/89	16
1983/84	20	1989/90	18
1984/85	23	1990/91	28
1985/86	22		

DANNY FOWLER

World ranking: Number 29
Date of birth: 30 July 1956
Star sign: Leo

Prize money 1989/90: £46,802.50
Turned professional: 1984
Country: England

No rubbish: Danny Fowler, the former dustman from Worksop, reached two semi-finals and came into the top thirty-two at number 29.

Danny Fowler's season virtually centred around two tournaments – the Rothmans Grand Prix and the Dubai Duty Free Classic. This former dustman and miner from Worksop reached the semi-finals of both tournaments and the points he gained clinched his move into the top thirty-two. But Fowler, one of the game's most popular players, was unable to maintain his form in the second half of the season after personal tragedy struck his career. His manager and friend, Tony Goulding, was killed in a car crash and understandably Fowler's results reflected his personal grief. This season he will be looking to recapture his form and perhaps move towards a top-sixteen position.

BEST PERFORMANCES

Embassy World Championship:
Round 1 1986 (lost to Terry Griffiths 10–2)
Round 1 1988 (lost to Tony Knowles 10–8)
Round 1 1990 (lost to Jimmy White 10–4)

Other Ranking Tournaments
Hong Kong Open:
Round 3 1989 (lost to Mike Hallett 5–2)
555 Asian Open:
Round 3 1989 (lost to Joe Johnson 5–4)
BCE International:
Round 1 (last 32) 1984 (lost to Dean Reynolds 5–2)
Rothmans Grand Prix:
Semi-finalist 1989 (lost to Steve Davis 9–2)
Dubai Duty Free Classic:
Semi-finalist 1989 (lost to Stephen Hendry 5–4)

StormSeal UK Open:
Round 5 1987 (lost to Mike Hallett 9–4)
Round 5 1988 (lost to Steve Davis 9–6)
Mercantile Credit Classic:
Round 5 1987 (lost to Stephen Hendry 5–4)
Pearl Assurance British Open:
Round 2 (last 32) 1985 (lost to Malcolm Bradley 5–4)
European Open:
Round 5 1989 (lost to Jim Wych 5–4)

Other Wins
No significant wins

World Ranking Positions

1985/86	55	1988/89	43
1986/87	33	1989/90	36
1987/88	40	1990/91	29

TONY DRAGO

World ranking: Number 30
Date of birth: 22 September 1965
Star sign: Virgo

Prize money 1989/90: £33,077.75
Turned professional: 1985
Country: Malta

Tony Drago went through a season he would rather forget and just stayed in the world's top thirty-two. He reached the last sixteen in the 555 Asian Open, the Dubai Duty Free Classic and the Mercantile Credit Classic, but did not manage to progress any further. There was also disappointment in the British Car Rental World Cup when Drago and his Rest of the World squad were beaten 5–2 by Northern Ireland in the first round – two years ago he had produced a brilliant performance in taking the Rest of the World to the final. In the Embassy World Championship, Drago was hammered 10–4 by Willie Thorne in the first round, and he will this season be looking to make a long-awaited step into the top sixteen. He is a snooker world record holder, having won a frame against Danny Fowler in the Fidelity Unit Trusts International in 1988 in just three minutes.

BEST PERFORMANCES

Embassy World Championship:
Quarter-finalist 1988 (lost to Steve Davis 13–4)

Other Ranking Tournaments
Hong Kong Open:
Round 3 1989 (lost to Marcel Gauvreau 5–0)
555 Asian Open:
Round 5 1989 (lost to Terry Griffiths 5–3)
BCE International:
Round 4 1986 (lost to Bob Chaperon 5–1)
Round 4 1989 (lost to John Parrott 5–3)
Rothmans Grand Prix:
Round 5 1985 (lost to Cliff Wilson 5–2)
Round 5 1987 (lost to Willie Thorne 5–2)
Dubai Duty Free Classic:
Round 5 1989 (lost to Stephen Hendry 5–3)
StormSeal UK Open:
Quarter-finalist 1986 (lost to Steve Davis 9–8)

Mercantile Credit Classic:
Round 5 1990 (lost to Steve Davis 5–3)
Pearl Assurance British Open:
Round 4 1989 (lost to Joe Johnson 5–3)
Round 4 1990 (lost to Neal Foulds 5–0)
European Open:
Round 3 1989 (lost to Mark Bennett 5–1)
Round 3 1990 (lost to Nigel Bond 5–2)

Other Wins	World Ranking Positions			
Malta Amateur: 1984	1986/87	37	1989/90	30
	1987/88	32	1990/91	30
	1988/89	20		

EDDIE CHARLTON

World ranking: Number 31
Date of birth: 31 October 1929
Star sign: Scorpio

Prize money 1989/90: £29,015.00
Turned professional: 1960
Country: Australia

Eddie Charlton, now sixty-one, managed to hang on to his place in the world's top thirty-two but it was a bit of a struggle for the tough-playing and tough-talking Australian. He has had a remarkable career but has never captured one of the game's major honours, though he twice finished runner-up in the World Championship in 1973 and 1975. Last season Charlton, who still jogs 6 miles a day, reached the last sixteen of only one tournament – the European Open in Lyon – where he was beaten 5–2 by Doug Mountjoy. In the World Championship he lost in the first round 10–1 to Steve Davis. He holds a place in the snooker records with the second-latest finish to a match – at 2.39am – when he beat Cliff Thorburn 10–9 in the first round of the World Championship in 1989.

BEST PERFORMANCES

Embassy World Championship:
Runner-up 1973 (lost to Ray Reardon 38–32)
Runner-up 1975 (lost to Ray Reardon 31–30)

Other Ranking Tournaments
Hong Kong Open:
Round 4 1989 (lost to Jimmy White 5–2)
555 Asian Open:
Round 3 1989 (lost to Gary Wilkinosn 5–3)
BCE International:
Semi-finalist 1983 (lost to Steve Davis 9–2)
Rothmans Grand Prix:
Semi-finalist 1982 (lost to Ray Reardon 10–7)
Dubai Duty Free Classic:
Round 4 1989 (lost to David Roe 5–3)
StormSeal UK Open:
Round 2 (last 16) 1984 (lost to Willie Thorne 9–7)
Mercantile Credit Classic:
Quarter-finalist 1984 (lost to Mark Wildman 5–4)
Pearl Assurance British Open:
Round 5 1986 (lost to John Virgo 5–4)
European Open:
Quarter-finalist 1989 (lost to John Parrott 5–1)

Current Non-ranking Tournaments
Benson and Hedges Masters:
Semi-finalist 1975 (lost to John Spencer 5–2)
Semi-finalist 1976 (lost to Ray Reardon 5–4)
Semi-finalist 1983 (lost to Cliff Thorburn 6–5)
Benson and Hedges Irish Masters:
Quarter-finalist 1983 (lost to Steve Davis 5–1)
Quarter-finalist 1985 (lost to Tony Knowles 5–3)

Other Wins
Pot Black: 1972, 1973, 1980
World Matchplay: 1976
Limosin International: 1979
Kronenbrau 1308 Classic: 1979
Australian Professional: 1964-67, 1969-84

World Ranking Positions

1976/77	3	1984/85	6
1977/78	3	1985/86	12
1978/79	3	1986/87	25
1979/80	3	1987/88	26
1980/81	3	1988/89	19
1981/82	8	1989/90	22
1982/83	5	1990/91	31
1983/84	6		

JAMES WATTANA

World ranking: Number 32
Date of birth: 17 January 1970
Star sign: Capricorn

Prize money 1989/90: £64,321.50
Turned professional: 1989
Country: Thailand

James Wattana arrived on the professional scene amidst a blaze of publicity. He was the world amateur titleholder, an exciting and fast potter, and was being hailed as a future world champion. The pressure of leaving his native Thailand and living in Britain might have proved too much for him, but he coped admirably with the demands and, after just one season, has come into the top thirty-two. Of course, he was originally number 33, but the disciplinary problems of Alex Higgins meant a rise of one place. Wattana made a brilliant start to his career when he reached the final of the 555 Asian Open in his native Bangkok where, after an exceptional match, he was beaten 9–6 by Stephen Hendry. He also reached the semi-final of the Rothmans Grand Prix and, although the remainder of the season might have been a shade disappointing, he could look back on his first campaign with pride.

BEST PERFORMANCES

Embassy World Championship:
Fifth qualifying round 1990 (lost to Alex Higgins 10–6)

Other Ranking Tournaments
Hong Kong Open:
Round 2 1989 (lost to Ian Graham 5–4)
555 Asian Open:
Runner-up 1989 (lost to Stephen Hendry 9–6)
BCE International:
Round 4 1989 (lost to Stephen Hendry 5–3)
Rothmans Grand Prix:
Semi-finalist 1989 (lost to Dean Reynolds 9–8)
Dubai Duty Free Classic:
Round 4 1989 (lost to John Parrott 5–3)
StormSeal UK Open:
Round 3 1989 (lost to Mike Hallett 9–7)
Mercantile Credit Classic:
Round 2 1990 (lost to Darren Morgan 5–1)
Pearl Assurance British Open:
Round 4 1990 (lost to Tony Knowles 5–3)
European Open:
Round 2 1990 (lost to Alain Robidoux 5–2)

Current Non-ranking Tournaments
Benson and Hedges Masters:
Round 1 1990 (lost to Steve Davis 5–2)

Other Wins
Camus Masters: 1986
Asian Amateur: 1986, 1988
World Amateur: 1988

World Ranking Positions
1989/90 –   1990/91 32

THE WAY THEY WERE . .

Well-groomed and assured . . . that's the television image of today's top snooker players. But wait a minute — what did these immaculate professionals look like in their formative years? The *Benson and Hedges Snooker Year* has been peering into the family scrapbooks of some of the most famous names in the game — with surprising results! Seven top players have given us permission to show *Snooker Year* readers

①

②

③

BUT WHO ARE THEY?

what they looked like as children: can you tell who they are?

Just study the seven pictures carefully and work out who is who. It's not easy, and we are certain many of you will be baffled. And don't forget: no cheating . . . even though we have put the answers on page 140. If you get all seven we reckon you are a genius, and anyone who gets four right is doing pretty well.

⑥

④

⑤

⑦

REFLECTIONS ON A TOURNAMENT YEAR

LION BROWN MASTERS

Willie Thorne captured his first title for three years as he earned the £11,538 first prize in the Lion Brown Masters in the unique snooker surroundings of the Legislative Council Chambers of the House of Parliament in Wellington, New Zealand. The world number 9 was delighted to find his touch again and revealed that being 'warned off' British racecourses was the factor that helped his success. (He had been in trouble for non-payment of training fees for his horses.)

Thorne had a remarkable run to the final and in the first round knocked in breaks of 53 and 89 for a 6–5 victory over Dennis Taylor after being 5–4 behind. Then, in the semi-final, he met defending champion Stephen Hendry who had come through by beating local favourite Dene O'Kane 6–3.

The Thorne v. Hendry match was voted the greatest ever seen in New Zealand and at the interval Thorne led 3–2 with breaks of 53, 75 and 137. After the break Hendry, who had already scored a 76 and a 56, fired in breaks of 89 and 55 while taking three frames to lead 5–3. But then Thorne knocked in a 120 in the ninth frame, won a tough tenth, and a break of 67 put him through to the final 6–5.

Joe Johnson, who had put out Mike Hallet and Tony Knowles, was waiting for Thorne in the final, but it was Leicester man Thorne who came through to victory with a score of 7–4.

Lion Brown Masters Results

FIRST ROUND:	A. Knowles (Eng) bt J. Parrott (Eng) 6–3; J. Johnson (Eng) bt M. Hallett (Eng) 6–5; W. Thorne (Eng) bt Dennis Taylor (NI) 6–5; S. Hendry (Scot) bt D. O'Kane (NZ) 6–3 Losers: £3,461.54
SEMI-FINALS:	Johnson bt Knowles 6–3; Thorne bt Hendry 6–5
3RD/4TH PLAY-OFF:	Knowles bt Hendry 6–3 Loser: £4,230.77 Winner: £5,000
FINAL:	Thorne bt Johnson 7–4 Loser: £7,692.31 Winner: £11,538.46

High break: 137 – W. Thorne £961.54

Previous Years' Results

YEAR	WINNER	RUNNER-UP	SCORE
1989	S. Hendry (Scot)	M. Hallett (Eng)	6–1

HONG KONG OPEN

Mike Hallett earned his first ranking tournament title since turning professional in 1979 when he came from behind to beat New Zealand's Dene O'Kane 9–8 to collect the £40,000 first prize in the Hong Kong Open. Hallett, who had taken the English title earlier in the year, led 4–3 but then trailed 8–6 as O'Kane looked certain to become the first overseas winner of a ranking title since Cliff Thorburn in 1985. But a determined Hallett won the last three frames to prove he could be a big-time winner.

At the start of 1988 Hallett had lost 9–0 to Steve Davis in the final of the Benson and Hedges Masters and had then twice been crushed by Stephen Hendry – 13–2 in the final of the British Open and 6–1 in the final of the Lion Brown Masters. To complete the bad spell there was also a beating by Davis in the Embassy World Championship.

Hallett said: 'Ian Doyle convinced me I could be a winner, that I could win a major title. I owe Ian a great debt. At 8–6 I thought I was out of it, beaten. But I stuck at it and I have been waiting a long, long time for this victory. I had been saying to myself: "Is it ever going to happen to me?" It has now.' O'Kane, after his first final, said: 'I didn't lose it, Mike won it.'

Hallett had been delighted with his 5–4 defeat of Stephen Hendry in the quarter-final and then he destroyed Jimmy White 5–2 in the semi-final after a match that had lasted just 93 minutes. In the other semi-final, Gary Wilkinson, who had knocked out Irishman Dennis Taylor in the quarter-final, came unstuck 5–3 against O'Kane.

The Hong Kong Open was the first ranking tournament to be held in this British colony and, despite a few hiccups, proved to be a success. The only drawback was a lack of adequate places for the spectators in the early rounds.

The star attraction: Mike Hallett is interviewed by the local media after beating Dene O'Kane 9-8 to win the Hong Kong Open.

Hong Kong Open Results

FOURTH ROUND		FIFTH ROUND		QUARTER-FINALS		SEMI-FINALS		FINAL	
J. Parrott (Eng)	2								
v		Newbury	1						
S. Newbury (Wales)	5			Gary Wilkinson	5				
Gary Wilkinson (Eng)	5	v							
v		Gary Wilkinson	5						
B. Pinches (Eng)	4			v		Gary Wilkinson	3		
M. Clark (Eng)	5								
v		Clark	3						
R. Chaperon (Can)	2	v		Dennis Taylor	3				
Dennis Taylor (NI)	5								
v		Dennis Taylor	5						
B. Gollan (Can)	4					v		O'Kane	8
A. Jones (Eng)	5								
v		A. Jones	3						
D. Roe (Eng)	1	v		Graham	1				
S. James (Eng)	3								
v		Graham	5						
I. Graham (Eng)	5			v		O'Kane	5		
A. Meo (Eng)	4								
v		Higgins	2						
A. Higgins (NI)	5	v		O'Kane	5				
T. Griffiths (Wales)	4								
v		O'Kane	5						
D. O'Kane (NZ)	5							v	
J. White (Eng)	5								
v		White	5						
E. Charlton (Aust)	2	v		White	5				
D. Mountjoy (Wales)	w/o								
v		Mountjoy	3						
C. Wilson (Wales)				v		White	2		
J. Chambers (Eng)	0								
v		N. Foulds	5						
N. Foulds (Eng)	5	v		N. Foulds	2				
W. Thorne (Eng)	5								
v		Thorne	1						
W. Jones (Wales)	1					v		Hallett	9
M. Hallett (Eng)	5								
v		Hallett	5						
B. West (Eng)	4	v		Hallett	5				
J. Virgo (Eng)	5								
v		Virgo	1						
M. Gauvreau (Can)	2			v		Hallett	5		
L. Dodd (Eng)	5								
v		Dodd	3						
B. Morgan (Eng)	2	v		Hendry	4				
S. Hendry (Scot)	5								
v		Hendry	5						
A. Robidoux (Can)	4								

Losers: £2,500

Losers: £3,750

Losers: £6,000

Losers: £12,000

Loser: £22,500
Winner: £40,000

High break: 100 – D. O'Kane £2,500

555 ASIAN OPEN

The 555 Asian Open, held in the teeming city of Bangkok, was guaranteed to be a media success as soon as Thailand's local hero, James Wattana, qualified for the final stages at the Channel 9 Studio. Wattana, then nineteen, was such a celebrity that the Thai government cancelled the main news at night so that his twenty-five million fans could watch him perform live on television. Of course there was the problem that Wattana could have gone out in his first match, but that didn't happen, and the man they call 'Tong' surprised everybody – perhaps even himself – by reaching the final. Wattana beat Mike Hallett 5–3, Doug Mountjoy 5–2, Silvino Francisco 5–2, and then whitewashed the evergreen Terry Griffiths 5–0 in the semi-final.

Waiting for Wattana in the final was Stephen Hendry who knew he would go to number 1 in the provisional world rankings if he came home a winner and took the £40,000 first prize. The television audience was treated to a classic final that Hendry won 9–6 after a snooker spectacular lasting just 165 minutes. The young Scot was the favourite, firing in outstanding breaks of 41, 137, 140 and then 68 to take a 4–0 lead. That break of 140 gave Hendry the high break prize as well. The break building was of the highest quality as Hendry finished the first session 5–2 ahead and then in the evening knocked in a 115 to make it 6–2. The next four frames followed at breakneck speed as he went 8–4 in front. But Wattana proved that he is going to be a potent force in years to come as he fought back to 8–6 before Hendry took the fifteenth frame and the title with a break of 79.

'It's great to be number 1 in the provisional rankings for the first time,' he said, while Wattana, £22,500 richer, commented: 'It all came down to my safety game which just wasn't good enough.'

In the semi-finals Hendry had scraped home 5–4 against Gary Wilkinson as Wilkinson got a 'kick' in the last frame. It was the first time a ranking tournament had been held in Bangkok and overall the event was a success. But Wattana was the man who kept the local interest high . . . especially when the Prime Minister stepped in to 'order' the locals to watch snooker!

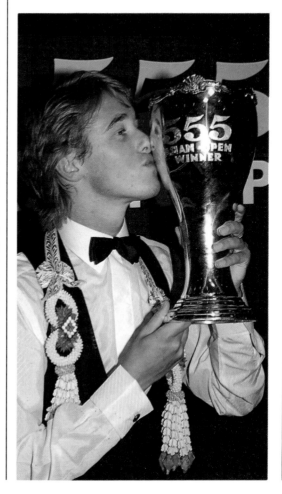

Seal of approval: Stephen Hendry kisses the trophy after overcoming James Wattana 9–6 in the final of the 555 Asian Open in Bangkok.

555 Asian Open Results

FOURTH ROUND		FIFTH ROUND		QUARTER-FINALS		SEMI-FINALS		FINAL	
I. Graham (Eng)	4								
v		S. Francisco	5						
S. Francisco (SA)	5								
		v		S. Francisco	2				
A. Knowles (Eng)	5								
v		Knowles	2						
N. Foulds (Eng)	3								
				v		Wattana	5		
D. Mountjoy (Wales)	5								
v		Mountjoy	2						
E. Hughes (Rep Ire)	4								
		v		Wattana	5				
M. Hallett (Eng)	3								
v		Wattana	5						
J. Wattana (Thai)	5								
						v		Wattana	6
A. Jones (Eng)	5								
v		A. Jones	5						
B. Oliver (Eng)	1								
		v		A. Jones	3				
S. James (Eng)	3								
v		Duggan	3						
S. Duggan (Eng)	5								
				v		Griffiths	0		
J. Johnson (Eng)	2								
v		Drago	3						
T. Drago (Malta)	5								
		v		Griffiths	5				
T. Griffiths (Wales)	5								
v		Griffiths	5						
D. Roe (Eng)	3								
								v	
C. Roscoe (Wales)	1								
v		P. Francisco	4						
P. Francisco (SA)	5								
		v		Gary Wilkinson	5				
A. Meo (Eng)	2								
v		Gary Wilkinson	5						
Gary Wilkinson (Eng)	5								
				v		Gary Wilkinson	4		
M. Clark (Eng)	5								
v		Clark	5						
W. King (Aust)	3								
		v		Clark	0				
D. Gilbert (Eng)	3								
v		West	0						
B. West (Eng)	5								
						v		Hendry	9
W. Thorne (Eng)	5								
v		Thorne	5						
B. Gollan (Can)	1								
		v		Thorne	2				
J. Virgo (Eng)	5								
v		Virgo	2						
D. O'Kane (NZ)	3								
				v		Hendry	5		
D. Reynolds (Eng)	2								
v		W. Jones	0						
W. Jones (Wales)	5								
		v		Hendry	5				
S. Hendry (Scot)	5								
v		Hendry	5						
A. Higgins (NI)	3								

Losers: £2,500   Losers: £3,750   Losers: £6,000   Losers: £12,000   Loser: £22,500
Winner: £40,000

High break: 140 – S. Hendry £2,500

REGAL MASTERS

Stephen Hendry, after four years as a professional, had never won a major title in his native Scotland. He ended that minor jinx in his life with a quite remarkable performance in the £86,000 Regal Masters at the Scottish Exhibition and Conference Centre in Glasgow. Of course, there was a packed house for the final to watch Hendry take on Welshman Terry Griffiths and there was nearly a moment of snooker history. Only two previous finals had ended in whitewashes and, inevitably, Steve Davis was the man who had caused them both – 9–0 against Dennis Taylor in the Jameson International in 1981 and 9–0 against Mike Hallett in the Benson and Hedges Masters in 1988. But Hendry produced snooker of near perfection as he went 8–0 ahead in the afternoon session and another 'whitewash' seemed on the cards. Griffiths, however, stopped the

embarrassment by winning the ninth frame on a respotted black. Hendry quickly took the tenth and then a total clearance of 132 enabled him to lift a trophy aloft in his homeland for the first time after a 10–1 success.

After his victory Hendry said: 'I have had some bad performances in front of my Scottish fans – in fact they have been disastrous. It was nice to play well up here.' The tournament had been master-minded by Hendry's manager, Ian Doyle, who was delighted with the final result.

Ten players took part and in the opening match Scottish champion John Rea beat Ireland's Dennis Taylor 6–5 only to be put out himself by Steve Davis in the quarter-finals. In the semi-finals Hendry beat John Parrott 6–4 and Griffiths demolished Davis 6–2. Davis said: 'I didn't play badly – it was just that Terry was devastating.'

Final pair: Winner Stephen Hendry and runner-up Terry Griffiths after the Regal Masters final.

Regal Masters Results

FIRST ROUND:	John Rea (Scot) bt Dennis Taylor (NI) 6–5; C. Thorburn (Can) bt M. Macleod (Scot) 6–2 Losers: £1,500
QUARTER-FINALS:	S. Davis (Eng) bt John Rea 6–2; T. Griffiths (Wales) bt J. White (Eng) 6–3; S. Hendry (Scot) bt M. Hallett (Eng) 6–1; J. Parrott (Eng) bt Thorburn 6–5 Losers: £3,750
SEMI-FINALS:	Griffiths bt S. Davis 6–2; Hendry bt Parrott 6–4 Losers: £8,000
FINAL:	Hendry bt Griffiths 10–1 Loser: £16,000 Winner: £32,500

High break: 134 – J. Parrott £3,500

BCE INTERNATIONAL

Steve Davis had spent his time on holiday in Antigua and New Orleans instead of travelling to the overseas ranking tournaments in Hong Kong and Thailand. But it was back to business as usual as Davis won the BCE International title for the sixth time in nine years at Trentham Gardens in Stoke-on-Trent.

There was a lot of pressure on Davis because Stephen Hendry had moved above him at number 1 in the provisional world rankings. Davis had insisted that the rankings didn't really matter; even so it was the first time he hadn't been number 1 since 1983. The man opposing Davis in the final was Hendry, but it was Davis who came home a 9–4 winner. He said: 'It was a great match and very nerve-wracking, and winning justified my decision not to play abroad. I may have been rusty, but it didn't show out there.'

It was a great final and, as Davis said, it was a pity that the ITV cameras had decided not to cover this opening tournament on the UK circuit.

The semi-finals had also produced some excellent games, with Davis needing more than four hours to beat the tough Canadian Alain Robidoux whom he jokingly described afterwards as like 'a giant redwood'.

First-year professional Nigel Bond was the surprise semi-finalist in the other half of the draw where he matched Hendry shot for shot before taking a 5–4 lead. Hendry responded with a 105 and then led 43–0 in the decider. Bond, showing no sign of nerves, replied with a 48 but then missed a simple red into the middle for Hendry to return with a break of 43 to go through. An honest Hendry admitted: 'I thought I was out, because the way Nigel was potting I didn't see him missing.'

Bond had thrashed John Parrott 5–2 in the quarter-final, while Robidoux had put out Jimmy White 5–4. The most eagerly watched match of the tournament was a fourth-round encounter between Hendry and James Wattana after their superb match in the final of the 555 Asian Open. In the end Hendry won 5–3.

BCE International Results

FOURTH ROUND		FIFTH ROUND		QUARTER-FINALS		SEMI-FINALS		FINAL	
S. Davis (Eng)	5								
v		S. Davis	5						
W. Jones (Wales)	2	v		S. Davis	5				
M. Bennett (Wales)	2	N. Foulds	3						
v				v		Davis	6		
N. Foulds (Eng)	5								
B. Morgan (Eng)	5	B. Morgan	5						
v		v		B. Morgan	2				
E. Hughes (Rep Ire)	3	Dennis Taylor	4						
Dennis Taylor (NI)	5							Davis	9
v						v			
M. Clark (Eng)	4								
T. Griffiths (Wales)	2	Newbury	2						
v		v		Robidoux	5				
S. Newbury (Wales)	5	Robidoux	5						
A. Robidoux (Can)	5								
v				v		Robidoux	3		
R. Bales (Eng)	1								
W. Thorne (Eng)	5	Thorne	1						
v		v		White	4				
B. West (Eng)	2	White	5						
J. White (Eng)	5								
v								v	
R. Chaperon (Scot)	3								
S. Hendry (Scot)	5	Hendry	5						
v		v		Hendry	5				
J. Wattana (Thai)	3	A. Jones	4						
A. Jones (Eng)	5								
v				v		Hendry	6		
M. Johnston-Allen (Eng)	2								
R. Marshall (Eng)	5	Marshall	3						
v		v		C. Wilson	2				
E. Charlton (Aust)	2	C. Wilson	5						
M. Hallett (Eng)	4								
v								Hendry	4
C. Wilson (Wales)	5						v			
N. Bond (Eng)	5	Bond	5						
v		v		Bond	5				
S. Francisco (SA)	3	James	0						
S. James (Eng)	5								
v				v		Bond	5		
M. Smith (Eng)	3								
A. Knowles (Eng)	5	Knowles	2						
v		v		Parrott	2				
A. Cairns (Eng)	2	Parrott	5						
J. Parrott (Eng)	5								
v									
A. Drago (Malta)	3								
Losers: £1,937.50		Losers: £3,000		Losers: £6,000		Losers: £12,000		Loser: £24,000	
								Winner: £40,000	

High break: 139 – J. Parrott £4,000

Previous Years' Results

YEAR	WINNER	RUNNER-UP	SCORE
1981	(Jameson) S. Davis (Eng)	Dennis Taylor (NI)	9–0
1982	(Jameson) A. Knowles (Eng)	David Taylor (Eng)	9–6
1983	(Jameson) S. Davis (Eng)	C. Thorburn (Can)	9–4
1984	(Jameson) S. Davis (Eng)	A. Knowles (Eng)	9–2
1985	(Goya) C. Thorburn (Can)	J. White (Eng)	12–10
1986	(BCE) N. Foulds (Eng)	C. Thorburn (Can)	12–9
1987	(Fidelity) S. Davis (Eng)	C. Thorburn (Can)	12–5
1988	(Fidelity) S. Davis (Eng)	J. White (Eng)	12–6

First of the season: Steve Davis, who did not play in the first two ranking events, came out on top in the BCE International in Stoke-on-Trent.

ROTHMANS GRAND PRIX

Steve Davis must be almost fed up with setting new records in snooker but he did it again in the Rothmans Grand Prix final at Reading when he overwhelmed Dean Reynolds 10–0. It was the biggest whitewash in the history of the game.

Davis' embarrassingly easy victory proved to be another landmark when the record books were checked and it was discovered that this Grand Prix success was the fiftieth major title of his career.

He said afterwards: 'I don't enjoy humiliating players but I took great pride in my performance for being able to maintain such a high standard throughout.' Reynolds would only comment: 'I would not say he is the best player in the world – there are several players equally as good, although his record does prove otherwise.'

The semi-final opponents for Davis and Reynolds had provided the media with quality copy in the shape of James Wattana and 'Dustbin' Danny Fowler. Wattana had already hammered Willie Thorne 5–3 from 3–1 down, overcome Paul Gibson 5–3 and then taken on Doug Mountjoy who had surprisingly beaten Stephen Hendry for the third successive time. Wattana's 5–2 defeat of Mountjoy took him into the semi-final where, after a quite remarkable match, he lost 9–8 to Reynolds. At one stage, though, Wattana looked home and dry as he led 7–3.

Whitewash: Steve Davis after retaining the Rothmans Grand Prix title with a 10–0 thrashing of Dean Reynolds in Reading.

Looking back: A dejected Dean Reynolds after his 10–0 final defeat by Steve Davis in the Rothmans Grand Prix.

Rothmans Grand Prix Results

FOURTH ROUND		FIFTH ROUND		QUARTER-FINALS		SEMI-FINALS		FINAL	
S. Davis (Eng)	5								
v		S. Davis	5						
N. Foulds (Eng)	4			S. Davis	5				
A. Meo (Eng)	3								
v		J. Smith	1						
J. Smith (Eng)	5					S. Davis	9		
A. Knowles (Eng)	5								
v		Knowles	5						
M. Clark (Eng)	2			Knowles	2				
C. Thorburn (Can)	4								
v		A. Jones	4						
A. Jones (Eng)	5							S. Davis	10
M. Hallett (Eng)	3								
v		Fowler	5						
D. Fowler (Eng)	5			Fowler	5				
A. Robidoux (Can)	5								
v		Robidoux	4						
E. Hughes (Rep Ire)	1					Fowler	2		
J. Johnson (Eng)	5								
v		Johnson	5						
A. Higgins (NI)	2			Johnson	4				
J. White (Eng)	5								
v		White	0						
J. Chambers (Eng)	1							v	
S. Hendry (Scot)	5								
v		Hendry	3						
N. Bond (Eng)	1			Mountjoy	2				
D. Mountjoy (Wales)	5								
v		Mountjoy	5						
M. Morra (Can)	0					Wattana	8		
W. Thorne (Eng)	3								
v		Wattana	5						
J. Wattana (Thai)	5			Wattana	5				
P. Gibson (Eng)	5								
v		P. Gibson	3						
L. Dodd (Eng)	4							Reynolds	0
Dennis Taylor (NI)	5								
v		Dennis Taylor	5						
B. Rowswell (Eng)	2			Dennis Taylor	3				
J. Virgo (Eng)	0								
v		Newbury	1						
S. Newbury (Wales)	5					Reynolds	9		
D. Reynolds (Eng)	5								
v		Reynolds	5						
W. King (Aust)	3			Reynolds	5				
J. Parrott (Eng)	5								
v		Parrott	2						
Gary Wilkinson (Eng)	1								
Losers: £3,390.62		Losers: £5,250		Losers: £10,500		Losers: £21,000		Loser: £42,000	
								Winner: £70,000	

High break: 138 – J. Johnson, J. White £7,000 (shared)

Previous Years' Results

YEAR	WINNER	RUNNER-UP	SCORE
1982	(Professional Players Tournament)		
	R. Reardon (Wales)	J. White (Eng)	10–5
1983	(PPT)		
	A. Knowles (Eng)	J. Johnson (Eng)	9–8
1984	Dennis Taylor (NI)	C. Thorburn (Can)	10–2
1985	S. Davis (Eng)	Dennis Taylor (NI)	10–9
1986	J. White (Eng)	R. Williams (Eng)	10–6
1987	S. Hendry (Scot)	Dennis Taylor (NI)	10–7
1988	S. Davis (Eng)	A. Higgins (NI)	10–6

Fowler used to be a dustman and a miner but was persuaded to take the full-time plunge into professional snooker by his wife Sally. The £21,000 loser's cheque more than made up for a 9–2 mauling from Davis in the semi-final. On his way to the last four Fowler had beaten David Roe, Mike Hallett, Alain Robidoux and then Joe Johnson. A year earlier he had gone home after losing 5–0 in the third round to Jimmy White, a match that lasted a mere 53 minutes and is still listed in the record books as the world's fastest nine-frame match.

DUBAI DUTY FREE CLASSIC

Snooker in the desert seems as unnatural as tennis at the North Pole but there was no doubting that the Dubai Duty Free Classic was an outstanding success. Dubai, one of the United Arab Emirates, had hosted an eight-man tournament a year earlier, but this was the first time a full-blooded ranking event had come to the Middle East. With temperatures soaring over 100° Fahrenheit, players were grateful for the air-conditioned splendour of their hotel and the venue – the Al Nasr Stadium.

In the final Stephen Hendry was crowned the Desert King as he thrashed Welshman Doug Mountjoy 9–2, a performance that lifted him back to number 1 in the provisional rankings. It was a one-sided final as Hendry compiled seven breaks of more than 60 and was a worthy winner of the trophy presented by Sheikh Ahmed Bin Saeed Al Maktoum, a member of the ruling family.

Even so, Hendry should not have even been in the final as he had won his semi-final 5–4 against Danny Fowler with a fluke in the final frame. Fowler, 4–2 down, hit back to level at 4–4 with breaks of 65 and 61. Then in the decider Hendry, 60–1 ahead with 59 on the table, was pegged back to 60–38 and faced with what

King of the desert: Stephen Hendry holds aloft the elegant trophy after winning the Dubai Duty Free Classic.

Dubai Duty Free Classic Results

FOURTH ROUND		FIFTH ROUND		QUARTER-FINALS		SEMI-FINALS		FINAL	
J. Parrott (Eng)	5								
v		Parrott	5						
J. Wattana (Thai)	3			Parrott	5				
S. James (Eng)	5								
v		James	3						
J. Chambers (Eng)	4					Parrott	4		
P. Medati (Eng)	1			v					
v		P. Francisco	5						
P. Francisco (SA)	5			P. Francisco	1				
N. Bond (Eng)	5								
v		Bond	4					Mountjoy	2
A. Robidoux (Can)	4					v			
J. Grech (Malta)	5								
v		Grech	4						
Gary Wilkinson (Eng)	2			Higgins	2				
A. Higgins (NI)	5								
v		Higgins	5			Mountjoy	5		
D. O'Kane (NZ)	3			v					
E. Charlton (Aust)	3								
v		Roe	4						
D. Roe (Eng)	5			Mountjoy	5				
D. Mountjoy (Wales)	5								
v		Mountjoy	5					v	
W. King (Aust)	2								
A. Jones (Eng)	4								
v		Fowler	5						
D. Fowler (Eng)	5			Fowler	5				
M. Clark (Eng)	5								
v		Clark	3			Fowler	4		
B. Rowswell (Eng)	4			v					
J. Campbell (Aust)	1								
v		J. McLaughlin	5						
J. McLaughlin (NI)	5			J. McLaughlin	1				
J. Virgo (Eng)	5								
v		Virgo	4					Hendry	9
A. Chappel (Wales)	4					v			
D. Reynolds (Eng)	5								
v		Reynolds	5						
J. Spencer (Eng)	4			Reynolds	3				
B. West (Eng)	5								
v		West	2			Hendry	5		
W. Jones (Wales)	2			v					
C. Wilson (Wales)	0								
v		Drago	3						
A. Drago (Malta)	5			Hendry	5				
S. Hendry (Scot)	w/o								
v		Hendry	5						
J. Wych (Can)									
Losers: £2,500		Losers: £3,750		Losers: £6,000		Losers: £12,000		Loser: £22,500	
								Winner: £40,000	

High break: 105 – S. Hendry £2,500

seemed a perfect snooker on the brown. He not only escaped from the snooker but also fluked the brown in as well to win the match.

Afterwards Hendry remarked: 'I didn't deserve to win and the only thing I could say to Danny was "Sorry." '

Mountjoy had also needed a last-frame success in his 5–4 defeat of Parrott.

One of the surprise successes was Malta's Joe Grech, who used to earn his living as a

motorcycle dispatch rider. He battled through to the last sixteen only to lose 5–4 to Alex Higgins when he went in off the final brown in the final frame.

STORMSEAL UK OPEN

Steve Davis had virtually 'owned' the UK Open title during the 1980s but there were two new names on the trophy last season. StormSeal were the new sponsors for the second most important tournament on the circuit, and it was Stephen Hendry who came through superbly to beat Davis 16–12 in a magnificent final, for a first prize of £100,000.

Davis, 4–0 down, had recovered to 11–10 behind, but Hendry hammered in successive centuries of 123 and 112 and eventually took the title even though Davis scored a tournament-best 138 to collect the £8,000 high break prize.

'It means everything to me to beat Davis over a long distance,' said Hendry. 'I have always felt capable of doing it and now I have proved it to the disbelievers who thought Davis was in a different class from me in a long match.'

Davis was full of praise for his vanquisher: 'I think of Stephen as a truly great player and he has got a much better all-round game than any other challenger.'

Remarkably, both players could have found themselves out of the tournament before the final. Hendry scraped home 9–8 against Dean Reynolds in the fifth round and then squeezed out Terry Griffiths 9–7 in the semi-final. But the biggest shock was nearly reserved for Davis in his semi-final against Gary Wilkinson who had surprised everybody with a 9–0 whitewash of Jimmy White in the quarter-finals. Davis trailed 6–2 and then 8–7 before Wilkinson committed the biggest blunder of his snooker life. With only pink and black on the table in frame 16, Davis needed two snookers. He got one but Wilkinson thought that Davis could win by taking the final two colours and promptly tried to hit the pink thinly and missed. Davis quickly mopped up to make it 8–8 and won the next frame to go through to the final.

Doug Mountjoy, the defending champion, failed to survive the first day as he was beaten by Joe O'Boye 9–8.

Star-studded trio: (left to right) Steve Davis, Sir Matt Busby, the former manager of Manchester United, and Tom Finney, one of England's greatest footballers, during the launch of the StormSeal UK Open.

StormSeal UK Open Results

FOURTH ROUND		FIFTH ROUND		QUARTER-FINALS		SEMI-FINALS		FINAL	
J. O'Boye (Eng)	5								
v		Gollan	5						
B. Gollan (Can)	9			Robidoux	2				
A. Robidoux (Can)	9								
v		Robidoux	9						
S. Francisco (SA)	3					Griffiths	7		
A. Knowles (Eng)	9			v					
v		Knowles	7						
A. Drago (Malta)	7			Griffiths	9				
T. Griffiths (Wales)	9								
v		Griffiths	9						
A. Jones (Eng)	8							Hendry	16
C. Thorburn (Can)	5					v			
v		P. Francisco	3						
P. Francisco (SA)	9			M. Bennett	2				
K. Stevens (Can)	2								
v		M. Bennett	9						
M. Bennett (Wales)	9					Hendry	9		
D. Reynolds (Eng)	9			v					
v		Reynolds	8						
W. Jones (Wales)	8			Hendry	9				
S. Hendry (Scot)	9								
v		Hendry	9						
B. West (Eng)	1							v	
J. Parrott (Eng)	9								
v		Parrott	6						
R. Chaperon (Can)	8			Gary Wilkinson	9				
B. Morgan (Eng)	6								
v		Gary Wilkinson	9						
Gary Wilkinson (Eng)	9					Gary Wilkinson	8		
J. Johnson (Eng)	9			v					
v		Johnson	6						
M. Clark (Eng)	6			White	0				
J. White (Eng)	9								
v		White	9						
N. Foulds (Eng)	5							S. Davis	12
M. Hallett (Eng)	9					v			
v		Hallett	9						
D. O'Kane (NZ)	0			Hallett	5				
Dennis Taylor (NI)	9								
v		Dennis Taylor	6						
R. Williams (Eng)	2					S. Davis	9		
W. Thorne (Eng)	9			v					
v		Thorne	4						
A. Higgins (NI)	3			S. Davis	9				
S. Davis (Eng)	9								
v		S. Davis	9						
C. Wilson (Wales)	3								
Losers: £3,875		Losers: £6,000		Losers: £12,000		Losers: £24,000		Loser: £48,000	
								Winner: £100,000	

High break: 138 – S. Davis £8,000

Previous Years' Results

YEAR	WINNER	RUNNER-UP	SCORE
1977	(Super Crystalate) P. Fagan (Rep Ire)	D. Mountjoy (Wales)	12–9
1978	(Coral) D. Mountjoy (Wales)	David Taylor (Eng)	15–9
1979	(Coral) J. Virgo (Eng)	T. Griffiths (Wales)	14–13
1980	(Coral) S. Davis (Eng)	A. Higgins (NI)	16–6
1981	(Coral) S. Davis (Eng)	T. Griffiths (Wales)	16–3
1982	(Coral) T. Griffiths (Wales)	A. Higgins (NI)	16–15
1983	(Coral) A. Higgins (NI)	S. Davis (Eng)	16–15
1984	(Coral) S. Davis (Eng)	A. Higgins (NI)	16–8
1985	(Coral) S. Davis (Eng)	W. Thorne (Eng)	16–14
1986	(Tennents) S. Davis (Eng)	N. Foulds (Eng)	16–7
1987	(Tennents) S. Davis (Eng)	J. White (Eng)	16–14
1988	(Tennents) D. Mountjoy (Wales)	S. Hendry (Scot)	16–12

EVEREST WORLD MATCHPLAY

Jimmy 'Whirlwind' White, despite being the world number 4, was being written off in some circles as a fading star while Stephen Hendry and Steve Davis threatened to dominate the season. But White won the final tournament of the 1980s – the Everest World Matchplay – with an exceptional 18–9 final defeat of John Parrott at the Brentwood Centre in Essex.

White's victory was worth £100,000 – the most he had earned at one tournament – and manager Barry Hearn was quick to

Family affair: Jimmy White and his family celebrate his £100,000 victory in the Everest World Matchplay.

add his comments as White's family clan celebrated in style. Hearn once declared that White gave him more sleepless nights than all his other players put together. He said: 'With Jimmy's ability it's nothing short of disgraceful that he hadn't won a tournament in the UK for nearly three years. He must be fed up with people talking about Davis and Hendry, but that's been his own fault because he has not been a winner. It's fitting he should be the player to win the last tournament of the 1980s and now the 1990s are down to him.'

The final had been extended to the World Championship distance of thirty-five frames. By the end of day 1 the scores were all square at 8–8. Parrott made a dramatic entrance on day 2 as he suffered a serious nosebleed which held the match up for nearly ten minutes. He said that the injury had not affected his performance, but White quickly went 11–8 in front, including a break of 117.

After that White was in total control and, in just thirty-eight minutes at night, took the three frames he needed for his 18–9 win. White commented: 'I have got my enthusiasm back and some of that's down to Stephen Hendry. I enjoy watching him and he is good for the game.'

Steve Davis, the defending champion, didn't last long, going out in his opening match to Dean Reynolds, while White nearly departed at the same stage as he trailed Doug Mountjoy 5–2. Seven frames later White had won 9–5.

The semi-finals were excellent affairs. Reynolds, 8–3 down against White, captured five frames in a row before losing 9–8, while Parrott, 5–0 and 8–6 behind against Hendry, won the final three frames, during which he made breaks of 84 and 74.

Everest World Matchplay Results

FIRST ROUND		QUARTER-FINALS		SEMI-FINALS		FINAL	
		S. Davis (Eng)	7				
D. Reynolds (Eng)	9	v		Reynolds	8		
v		Reynolds	9				
A. Meo (Eng)	7					White	18
				v			
D. Mountjoy (Wales)	9						
v		Mountjoy	5	White	9		
W. Thorne (Eng)	2	v					
		J. White (Eng)	9				
						v	
		S. Hendry (Scot)	9				
T. Griffiths (Wales)	9	v		Hendry	8		
v		Griffiths	3				
C. Thorburn (Can)	5					Parrott	9
				v			
M. Hallett (Eng)	6						
v		Dennis Taylor	6	Parrott	9		
Dennis Taylor (NI)	9	v					
		J. Parrott (Eng)	9				
Losers: £5,000		Losers: £10,000		Losers: £20,000		Loser: £40,000 Winner: £100,000	

High break: 129 – S. Hendry £10,000

Previous Years' Results

YEAR	WINNER	RUNNER-UP	SCORE
1988	S. Davis (Eng)	J. Parrott (Eng)	9–5

MERCANTILE CREDIT CLASSIC

The Norbreck Castle Hotel in Blackpool is what you would call a typical English summer-holiday hotel – big, friendly and close to the beach. It also doubled as the venue for the seemingly never-ending rounds of qualifying tournaments and the final stages of the Mercantile Credit Classic. The Classic always takes place in January and Blackpool at that time of year can be a daunting prospect as winter waves often crash over the sea-wall. It is the first tournament after the Christmas and New Year break and there are usually a lot of shock results. Last season's Classic was no exception as Steve James, the world number 16, fought his way through the field to take on Australian outsider Warren King, ranked number 55, in the final. In fact, only four of the top sixteen managed to reach the last sixteen.

James, a former postman, led 7–4 though King, a one-time bookie's runner

from Sydney, came back to 6–7 and seemed certain to take the fourteenth too as he led 58–0. However, James, one of the most exciting players in the game, won that frame with a 70 clearance and quickly took the two frames he needed for a 10–6 victory and a £60,000 pay day.

James had certainly enjoyed his 6–4 semi-final over Steve Davis – a performance that included a high-speed 141 that earned James a £6,000 bonus for the high break. He said: 'Beating Steve was important, but then I had to make sure I didn't forget that I had to win the final as well. If I had lost then, it would have meant I had thrown all the hard work away.'

King's final appearance came courtesy of a 6–5 victory over South African Silvino Francisco.

In the opening matches Doug Mountjoy, the defending champion, went down 5–4 to Steve Duggan, Jimmy White withdrew after catching flu and Joe Johnson was hammered 5–0 by Nigel Gilbert, the young man from Bedford who wears a white glove on his bridging hand to combat perspiration.

Stephen Hendry, who had dominated the first half of the season, was physically sick during the night and was even 'sicker' during the day when he lost 5–2 to Dene O'Kane in round 4. Hendry said: 'No excuses – Dene deserved to win.'

There were shocks and surprises right the way through, but in the end it was all down to James – the man they call the Cannock Cannonball. He rides high-powered motorbikes for fun, pots snooker balls for a living and drew this compliment from Davis: 'Steve is a very entertaining player and not as mad on the table as people used to think. He's great to watch.'

King James the First: Steve James holds high the Mercantile Credit Classic trophy – his first major title.

Mercantile Credit Classic Results

FOURTH ROUND

Player	Score
S. Duggan (Eng)	2
P. Francisco (SA)	5
A. Meo (Eng)	4
S. Newbury (Wales)	5
J. Virgo (Eng)	5
J. McLaughlin (NI)	2
W. King (Aust)	5
E. Charlton (Aust)	2
I. Brumby (Eng)	0
S. Francisco (SA)	5
D. Reynolds (Eng)	4
M. Rowing (Eng)	5
N. Gilbert (Eng)	2
M. Clark (Eng)	5
S. Hendry (Scot)	2
D. O'Kane (NZ)	5
J. Parrott (Eng)	5
A. Higgins (NI)	4
S. James (Eng)	5
R. Chaperon (Can)	2
J. Campbell (Aust)	4
Gary Wilkinson (Eng)	5
M. Hallett (Eng)	3
W. Jones (Wales)	5
C. Thorburn (Can)	4
D. Morgan (Wales)	5
David Taylor (Eng)	4
B. Morgan (Eng)	5
Dennis Taylor (NI)	4
A. Drago (Malta)	5
S. Davis (Eng)	5
R. Williams (Eng)	0

FIFTH ROUND

Player	Score
P. Francisco	3
Newbury	5
Virgo	1
King	5
S. Francisco	5
Rowing	1
Clark	1
O'Kane	5
Parrott	3
James	5
Gary Wilkinson	2
W. Jones	5
D. Morgan	1
B. Morgan	5
Drago	3
S. Davis	5

QUARTER-FINALS

Player	Score
Newbury	3
King	5
S. Francisco	5
O'Kane	4
James	5
W. Jones	2
B. Morgan	1
S. Davis	5

SEMI-FINALS

Player	Score
King	6
S. Francisco	5
James	6
S. Davis	4

FINAL

Player	Score
King	6
James	10

Losers: £2,906.25   Losers: £4,500   Losers: £9,000   Losers: £18,000   Loser: £36,000
Winner: £60,000

High break: 141 – S. James £6,000

Previous Years' Results

YEAR	WINNER	RUNNER-UP	SCORE
1980	(Wilsons Classic) J. Spencer (Eng)	A. Higgins (NI)	4–3
1981	(Wilsons Classic) S. Davis (Eng)	Dennis Taylor (NI)	4–1
1982	(Lada) T. Griffiths (Wales)	S. Davis (Eng)	9–8
1983	(Lada) S. Davis (Eng)	W. Werbeniuk (Can)	9–5
1984	(Lada) S. Davis (Eng)	A. Meo (Eng)	9–8
1985	W. Thorne (Eng)	C. Thorburn (Can)	13–8
1986	J. White (Eng)	C. Thorburn (Can)	13–12
1987	S. Davis (Eng)	J. White (Eng)	13–12
1988	S. Davis (Eng)	J. Parrott (Eng)	13–11
1989	D. Mountjoy (Wales)	W. Jones (Wales)	13–11

BENSON AND HEDGES MASTERS

Twelve months earlier Stephen Hendry had, at twenty, become the youngest-ever Benson and Hedges Masters champion. He returned to the Wembley Conference Centre and delighted a 2,740 crowd by retaining the title with a 9–4 victory over John Parrott.

Parrott had been Hendry's final opponent the previous year, but this time he had looked as though he was going to be a tougher prospect, especially after his 6–2 thrashing of Steve Davis in the semi-final. It was not to be and Hendry, narrowly missing a maximum 147 in the twelfth frame when he failed on the thirteenth black, competently took the £70,000 first prize.

'Hendry's long potting destroys people,' said a generous Parrott. 'Two years ago, if I had beaten Davis, I knew the rest would be easy. This time I knew I still had the hardest job to do. He's the best player in the world at the moment.'

Benson and Hedges had changed the tournament's format with the introduction of two 'wild cards' to add spice to the already star-studded line-up of the world's top sixteen players. Alex Higgins and James Wattana were the two players chosen. Higgins went out 5–2 to Steve James in the play-off round, while Wat-tana suffered a 5–2 first-round defeat by Davis after beating Dean Reynolds 5–4 in his opening match.

Wattana, the young Thai in his first season, had always looked up to Davis as his snooker idol. They had met once before when Davis was involved in a tournament-cum-exhibition in Bangkok. Wattana won 2–1, but here at Wembley was the first time they had met in a serious professional competition. Wattana's potting was fine; his safety play, however, left Davis far too many chances. The Thais, who do like a flutter, were even investing money in the match by telephone from Bangkok. In the end it was bookmakers Coral who cashed in.

The first semi-final featured Hendry and Jimmy White with White, 2–0 down, going 4–3 ahead. White could not maintain the momentum and Hendry easily collected the three frames he needed for a 6–4 success. Parrott, despite an equal tournament best by Davis of 111, was far too strong in the second quarter-final, though Parrott was worried at the end when he had to put on a new tip late at night. He admitted: 'I didn't have a suitable replacement and I had to sneak up to the trade exhibition stands at night to get a new tip.'

Hendry was putting his remarkable success down to the many hours he had spent at the practice table. He said: 'At one time, I was getting lazy and didn't realise how hard you had to work. But a couple of years ago my manager, Ian Doyle, gave me a kick up the backside and now I am practising six or seven hours a day.' Practice makes perfect, they say, and although Hendry is not yet perfect, he was certainly heading that way after his fifth success of the season.

Benson and Hedges Masters Results

PLAY-OFFS		FIRST ROUND		QUARTER-FINALS		SEMI-FINALS		FINAL	
		S. Hendry (Scot)	5						
S. James (Eng)	5	v		Hendry	5				
v		James	2						
A. Higgins (NI)	2			v		Hendry	6		
		W. Thorne (Eng)	5						
		v		Thorne	1				
		Dennis Taylor (NI)	4						
						v		Hendry	9
		T. Griffiths (Wales)	4						
		v		Knowles	3				
		A. Knowles (Eng)	5						
				v		White	4		
		J. Virgo (Eng)	3						
		v		White	5				
		J. White (Eng)	5						
								v	
		J. Parrott (Eng)	5						
		v		Parrott	5				
		A. Meo (Eng)	3						
				v		Parrott	6		
		J. Johnson (Eng)	5						
		v		Johnson	3				
		M. Hallett (Eng)	4						
						v		Parrott	4
		C. Thorburn (Can)	4						
		v		Mountjoy	0				
D. Reynolds (Eng)	4	D. Mountjoy (Wales)	5						
v		v		v		S. Davis	2		
J. Wattana (Thai)	5	Wattana	2						
		v		S. Davis	5				
		S. Davis (Eng)	5						
Losers: £5,000		Losers: £7,000		Losers: £13,000		Losers: £21,000		Loser: £38,000	
								Winner: £70,000	

High break: 111 – S. Davis, S. Hendry £7,000 (shared)

Previous Years' Results

YEAR	WINNER	RUNNER-UP	SCORE
1975	J. Spencer (Eng)	R. Reardon (Wales)	9–8
1976	R. Reardon (Wales)	G. Miles (Eng)	7–3
1977	D. Mountjoy (Wales)	R. Reardon (Wales)	7–6
1978	A. Higgins (NI)	C. Thorburn (Can)	7–5
1979	P. Mans (SA)	A. Higgins (NI)	8–4
1980	T. Griffiths (Wales)	A. Higgins (NI)	9–5
1981	A. Higgins (NI)	T. Griffiths (Wales)	9–6
1982	S. Davis (Eng)	T. Griffiths (Wales)	9–5
1983	C. Thorburn (Can)	R. Reardon (Wales)	9–7
1984	J. White (Eng)	T. Griffiths (Wales)	9–5
1985	C. Thorburn (Can)	D. Mountjoy (Wales)	9–6
1986	C. Thorburn (Can)	J. White (Eng)	9–5
1987	Dennis Taylor (NI)	A. Higgins (NI)	9–8
1988	S. Davis (Eng)	M. Hallett (Eng)	9–0
1989	S. Hendry (Scot)	J. Parrott (Eng)	9–6

PEARL ASSURANCE BRITISH OPEN

Canadian Bob Chaperon was one of the unsung heroes of the professional snooker circuit. He was a member of the top thirty-two, earned a reasonable yearly 'wage', scored the odd surprise victory over a top seeded player and yet never looked like winning a major title. That all changed at the Pearl Assurance British Open at the Assembly Rooms in Derby.

Chaperon, from Sudbury, British Ontario, was always known as a tough competitor, especially as he used to exist by hustling his way round the Canadian pool and snooker halls. The turning point came when the Gainsborough Snooker Club, close to where he now lives in England, installed a BCE Championship table similar to the one used in the major tournaments.

'I also had a new cue which cost me £130 and was brought over from Canada for me by Alain Robidoux. Three weeks before the British Open I told a club member that I would make a 147 and win a major title. I did the 147 a couple of days later and now I have got a title,' said Chaperon.

As the top players tumbled, Chaperon came through the pack to reach his first major final where he came up against a revitalised Alex 'Hurricane' Higgins. One cynic had pointed out that, in his opinion, Chaperon would never reach a final and Higgins would never reach another final. Chaperon v. Higgins proved that statement to be totally incorrect, even though before the start the bookies had made Chaperon a 150–1 outsider and Higgins a 100–1 chance.

Higgins, nervous and twitchy early on when he complained to referee Alan Chamberlain that Chaperon had been standing in his line of sight, came from 4–1 down to lead 5–4. But he never went in front again and Chaperon took the £75,000 first prize

with a 10–8 scoreline, leaving Higgins the consolation of the biggest pay day, at £45,000, of his long career.

The tournament, from the fourth round onwards, had been redrawn at random *à la* FA Cup and there were some interesting matches. Darren Morgan had beaten Stephen Hendry 5–4 and then came up against Steve Davis in round 4. Morgan knocked in successive centuries of 116 and 108, led 4–1, but eventually went down 5–4.

Final embrace: Winner Bob Chaperon (right) and Alex Higgins, the runner-up, after Chaperon's victory in the final of the Pearl Assurance British Open.

Davis went out in round 5 to Welshman Steve Newbury who in turn departed to another surprise performer, Robert Marshall, the world number 70. Marshall's hopes of reaching the final were ended 9–5 by Chaperon in the semi-final, while Higgins booked his place with a 9–3 defeat of Steve James, who revealed during the tournament that he was suffering from diabetes.

Pearl Assurance British Open Results
(Redrawn at random from fourth round onwards)

FOURTH ROUND		FIFTH ROUND		QUARTER-FINALS		SEMI-FINALS		FINAL	
E. Hughes (Rep Ire)	5								
v		Dennis Taylor	3						
R. Williams (Eng)	2								
		v		Clark	3				
R. Marshall (Eng)	5								
v		Clark	5						
J. Johnson (Eng)	4								
				v		Higgins	9		
T. Murphy (NI)	2								
v		E. Hughes	0						
S. Newbury (Wales)	5								
		v		Higgins	5				
P. Browne (Rep Ire)	2								
v		Marshall	5						
M. Clark (Eng)	5								
						v		Higgins	8
A. Higgins (NI)	5								
v		Chaperon	5						
M. Bennett (Wales)	2								
		v		Chaperon	5				
A. Robidoux (Can)	5								
v		Robidoux	4						
S. Duggan (Eng)	4								
				v		James	3		
D. Mountjoy (Wales)	5								
v		Mountjoy	3						
D. Reynolds (Eng)	2								
		v		N. Foulds	3				
A. Knowles (Eng)	5								
v		Higgins	5						
J. Wattana (Thai)	3								
N. Foulds (Eng)	5							v	
v		Dodd	5						
A. Drago (Malta)	0								
		v		Marshall	5				
M. Hallett (Eng)	3								
v		Knowles	4						
R. Chaperon (Can)	5								
				v		Chaperon	9		
S. Davis (Eng)	5								
v		Newbury	5						
D. Morgan (Wales)	4								
		v		Newbury	4				
T. Griffiths (Wales)	1								
v		S. Davis	2						
P. Francisco (SA)	5								
						v		Chaperon	10
A. Wilson (Eng)	0								
v		P. Francisco	3						
S. James (Eng)	5								
		v		Dodd	2				
Dennis Taylor (NI)	5								
v		N. Foulds	5						
M. Macleod (Scot)	2								
				v		Marshall	5		
J. White (Eng)	5								
v		James	5						
A. Meo (Eng)	0								
		v		James	5				
M. Rowing (Eng)	2								
v		White	4						
L. Dodd (Eng)	5								
Losers: £3,634		Losers: £5,625		Losers: £11,250		Losers: £22,500		Loser: £45,000	
								Winner: £75,000	

High break: 138 – J. White £7,500

Previous Years' Results

YEAR	WINNER	RUNNER-UP	SCORE
1980	(British Gold Cup) A. Higgins (NI)	R. Reardon (Wales)	5–1
1981	(Yamaha) S. Davis (Eng)	David Taylor (Eng)	9–6
1982	(Yamaha) S. Davis (Eng)	T. Griffiths (Wales)	9–7
1983	(Yamaha) R. Reardon (Wales)	J. White (Eng))	9–6
1984	(Yamaha) Three-man play-off		
	D. Martin (Eng)	J. Dunning (Eng)	3–2
	S. Davis (Eng)	J. Dunning	4–1
	S. Davis	D. Martin	3–0
	Winner – Davis		
1985	(Dulux) S. Francisco (SA)	K. Stevens (Can)	12–9
1986	(Dulux) S. Davis (Eng)	W. Thorne (Eng)	12–7
1987	(Dulux) J. White (Eng)	N. Foulds (Eng)	13–9
1988	(MIM Britannia) S. Hendry (Scot)	M. Hallett (Eng)	13–2
1989	(Anglian Windows) A. Meo (Eng)	D. Reynolds (Eng)	13–6

EUROPEAN OPEN

After the glamour of travelling to Hong Kong, Thailand and Dubai for the first three overseas ranking tournaments of the season, it was back to reality with a trip to the industrial city of Lyon in France for the European Open. This had been switched to Lyon following the disappointment in Deauville the previous year when so few people turned up to watch the inaugural tournament. Certainly attendances were better, and Canal Plus televison must have been happy with the quality of the final, played out at the Maison du Judo, when John Parrott retained his title by beating Stephen Hendry 10–6.

In nine previous finals Parrott had won only one, the 1989 European Open. Now he could say: 'That event last year didn't have any credibility because no one took the tournament seriously. But I have proved I can be a winner by beating the best player in the world.'

Parrott's only disappointment was the fact that he missed out on his annual three-day trip to his beloved Cheltenham Races, but the £40,000 winner's cheque helped compensate. He was delighted with playing some of the best snooker of his career: 'The way I was feeling out there, the only way Stephen could have beaten me was by physically knocking me out.'

Hendry admitted: 'I am just happy that John didn't slaughter me,' while in the semi-final the young Scot had comfortably disposed of Steve Davis 6–3. Parrott had overcome the dangerous Steve James by the same score.

There were some familiar faces in the quarter-finals but also two outsiders. Colin Roscoe, a former ice-cream salesman, had never tasted a place in a major quarter-final, yet he picked up £6,000 despite losing to James 5–2. Professional new boy Nigel Bond went down to Parrott 5–3 but he was still delighted with his victory in the previous round when he needed four snookers in the final frame against John Campbell and got them to win 5–4.

While Parrott missed out on his trip to the races, he certainly galloped to success in the final. His summing-up was perfect: 'Hendry is the most frightening, devastating player in the game and to beat him 10–6 was a tremendous achievement.'

European Open Results

FOURTH ROUND		FIFTH ROUND		QUARTER-FINALS		SEMI-FINALS		FINAL	
J. Parrott (Eng)	5								
v		Parrott	5						
W. Jones (Wales)	0			Parrott	5				
J. Johnson (Eng)	5	v							
v		Johnson	2						
D. Fowler (Eng)	1					Parrott	6		
D. Reynolds (Eng)	4			v					
v		Bond	5						
N. Bond (Eng)	5			Bond	3				
A. Robidoux (Can)	4	v							
v		J. Campbell	4						
J. Campbell (Aust)	5							Parrott	10
N. Dyson (Eng)	5					v			
v		Dyson	2						
M. Clark (Eng)	2			Roscoe	2				
J. Virgo (Eng)	2	v							
v		Roscoe	5						
C. Roscoe (Wales)	5					James	3		
S. James (Eng)	5			v					
v		James	5						
A. Higgins (NI)	2			James	5				
J. White (Eng)	5	v							
v		White	4					v	
D. Roe (Eng)	1								
S. Hendry (Scot)	5								
v		Hendry	5						
S. Newbury (Wales)	1			Hendry	5				
A. Chappel (Wales)	5	v							
v		Chappel	2						
David Taylor (Eng)	2					Hendry	6		
W. Thorne (Eng)	3			v					
v		N. Foulds	5						
N. Foulds (Eng)	5			N. Foulds	3				
M. Bennett (Wales)	5	v							
v		M. Bennett	2						
S. Francisco (SA)	3							Hendry	6
M. Price (Eng)	4					v			
v		Charlton	2						
E. Charlton (Aust)	5			Mountjoy	0				
D. Mountjoy (Wales)	5	v							
v		Mountjoy	5						
R. Williams (Eng)	0					S. Davis	3		
C. Edwards (Eng)	5			v					
v		Edwards	4						
D. O'Kane (NZ)	2			S. Davis	5				
S. Davis (Eng)	5	v							
v		S. Davis	5						
R. Chaperon (Can)	0								
Losers: £2,500		Losers: £3,750		Losers: £6,000		Losers: £12,000		Loser: £22,500	
								Winner: £40,000	

High break: 122 – S. James £2,500

Previous Years' Results

YEAR	WINNER	RUNNER-UP	SCORE
1989	(ICI) J. Parrott (Eng)	T. Griffiths (Wales)	9–8

BENSON AND HEDGES IRISH MASTERS

When Alex Higgins won the Benson and Hedges Irish Masters for the first time in 1989, a sell-out crowd acclaimed every shot as he beat Stephen Hendry 9–8 in a never-to-be-forgotten final. There was a standing-room-only crowd for the Hurricane's appearance at last season's Irish Masters, but this time the atmosphere was quite different. In fact, some might have described it as intimidating. Higgins was facing Dennis Taylor in a quarter-final that had made headline news after a serious clash between the two Irishmen at the World Cup final a week earlier. Then Higgins was alleged to have threatened to have Taylor 'shot' the next time he returned to Northern Ireland.

After Taylor's opening-round win against Cliff Thorburn, there was always going to be a lot of hostility in this quarter-final encounter. Taylor also claimed: 'Some of the things Higgins said to me at the World Cup were unprintable, but there was something said about my late mother Annie that will make me determined to beat him.' Even the normally non-commital Steve Davis had remarked: 'I will be out there watching because it could be the grudge match of all time.'

The venue was packed, the press seats were full up and ITN even talked to fans before the match to see which player they would be supporting.

Both players were introduced separately and both received an unbelievable welcome, Taylor's fans perhaps giving him the more enthusiastic reception. In the end it was Taylor who won 5–2 and he declared: 'I have never experienced an atmosphere like that even when I played Steve Davis in the 1985 World Championship final.'

Masterful: Steve Davis receives the Benson and Hedges Irish Masters trophy from Bert Koorn, the managing director of Gallaher (Dublin) Ltd.

That one match dominated the entire tournament, though Taylor got his mind back together to beat Jimmy White 6–5 from 3–0 and 5–3 down in the semi-final. By the final, however, Taylor was totally drained, and it was Steve Davis, without a tournament success for six events, who took the Irish Masters for the fifth time with a 9–4 victory.

Stephen Hendry, the game's in-form player, had been hammered by White 5–2 in the quarter-final, while Davis took care of Willie Thorne 5–3 and then Terry Griffiths 6–3.

Benson and Hedges Irish Masters Results

FIRST ROUND		QUARTER-FINALS		SEMI-FINALS		FINAL	
		A. Higgins (NI)	2				
C. Thorburn (Can)	3	v		Dennis Taylor	6		
v		Dennis Taylor	5				
Dennis Taylor (NI)	5						
				v		Dennis Taylor	4
J. White (Eng)	5						
v		White	5				
J. Johnson (Eng)	4	v		White	5		
		S. Hendry (Scot)	2				
						v	
		Griffiths	5				
T. Griffiths (Wales)	5	v		Griffiths	3		
v		J. Parrott (Eng)	3				
D. Mountjoy (Wales)	1						
				v		S. Davis	9
W. Thorne (Eng)	5						
v		Thorne	3				
M. Hallett (Eng)	1	v		S. Davis	6		
		S. Davis (Eng)	5				

Losers: £5,297.47   Losers: £8,186.99   Losers: £14,447.63   Loser: £22,153.04
                                                                                      Winner: £35,637.49

High break: 99 – W. Thorne, J. Parrott £3,852.70 (shared)

Previous Years' Results

YEAR	WINNER	RUNNER-UP	SCORE
1978	J. Spencer (Eng)	D. Mountjoy (Wales)	5–3
1979	D. Mountjoy (Wales)	R. Reardon (Wales)	6–5
1980	T. Griffiths (Wales)	D. Mountjoy (Wales)	9–8
1981	T. Griffiths (Wales)	R. Reardon (Wales)	9–7
1982	T. Griffiths (Wales)	S. Davis (Eng)	9–5
1983	S. Davis (Eng)	R. Reardon (Wales)	9–2
1984	S. Davis (Eng)	T. Griffiths (Wales)	9–1
1985	J. White (Eng)	A. Higgins (NI)	9–5
1986	J. White (Eng)	W. Thorne (Eng)	9–5
1987	S. Davis (Eng)	W. Thorne (Eng)	9–1
1988	S. Davis (Eng)	N. Foulds (Eng)	9–4
1989	A. Higgins (NI)	S. Hendry (Scot)	9–8

CONTINENTAL AIRLINES LONDON MASTERS

The Continental Airlines London Masters at the Cafe Royal in London holds a unique place in the tournament calendar. The tournament is spread over seven evenings during the winter and spring months and takes place in front of a dinner-jacketed audience following a lavish meal in one of the Cafe Royal's banqueting rooms.

The trophy also holds a unique place on the sideboard of Stephen Hendry who has now won it on both occasions. In 1989 he beat John Parrott 4–2 in the final and last season he repeated that feat to pick up the £30,000 first prize. It was Hendry's seventh major title of the season.

Eight players were invited and Steve Davis went out in the quarter-final 4–3 at the hands of Willie Thorne. Davis, despite being interrupted by a faulty fire alarm, led 3–2 and then looked on his way to victory in the deciding frame as he opened a lead of 53–0. But Thorne hit back with a break of 64 to go into the semi-final.

Hendry won his opening match 4–1 against Dennis Taylor, including a break of 100, while Parrott scored breaks of 104 and 130 in knocking out Hallett 4–1. That 130 break eventually earned Parrott the high break prize of £3,500, inspiring him to remark: 'I can't play much better than that.' The fourth quarter-final saw Jimmy White depart 4–2 at the hands of Tony Meo.

On to the semi-finals where Hendry, with a top score of 116, thrashed Meo 4–1 while Parrott overcame Thorne 4–2. In the end it was Hendry who went home a winner – just hours after signing a

Flying success: Stephen Hendry retained his title in the Continental Airlines London Masters.

£250,000 promotional deal with adhesive giants Bostik. Hendry will assist Bostik in advertising and also make twenty-one personal appearances which works out at roughly £12,000 a night.

Continental Airlines London Masters Results

FIRST ROUND:	W. Thorne (Eng) bt S. Davis (Eng) 4–3; S. Hendry (Scot) bt Dennis Taylor (NI) 4–1; J. Parrott (Eng) bt M. Hallett (Eng) 4–1; A. Meo (Eng) bt J. White (Eng) 4–2 Losers: £3,500
SEMI-FINALS:	Parrott bt Thorne 4–2; Hendry bt Meo 4–1 Losers: £7,500
FINAL:	Hendry bt Parrott 4–2 Loser: £12,500 Winner: £30,000

High break: 130 – J. Parrott £3,500

Previous Years' Results

YEAR	WINNER	RUNNER-UP	SCORE
1989	S. Hendry (Scot)	J. Parrott (Eng)	4–2

STORMSEAL MATCHROOM LEAGUE

Steve Davis might have lost his world title and world number 1 position last season, but there was no way he was going to relinquish his crown in the £220,000 Matchroom League, this time sponsored by StormSeal.

The toughest challenge to Davis winning his fourth League title in succession came from Stephen Hendry until the young Scot endured a disastrous spell . . . days after winning the World Championship. In the space of ten days Hendry played three matches and lost them all 5–3 – to John Parrott in Bury, Tony Meo in Burton-upon-Trent and Jimmy White in Oldham.

Davis, on the other hand, won five matches in a row and finally clinched the title and a £70,000 cheque when he thrashed Dennis Taylor 6–2 in Harrogate. There was one match left for Davis in Brentwood, just a few miles from his Essex farmhouse abode. The opponent was Hendry, who won 6–2, but the destination of the trophy was already decided.

The format of the League means that the bottom two players are relegated which results in a loss of pride as well as a loss in earnings. Last season there was a frantic struggle at the foot of the table to avoid the drop. In the end it was Parrott and Cliff Thorburn who found themselves out of the League after two fellow strugglers, White and Meo, obtained the point they needed for safety when they drew 4–4 with each other in Watford.

The only consolation for a bitterly disappointed Parrott was the high break prize of £5,000 for a 142 he made in the final frame of his excellent victory over Hendry. That 142 was also the highest break made in a professional tournament throughout the season.

The League has, at the time of writing, been guaranteed for another season. The format is refreshing as ten professionals play each other at various venues all over the UK.

StormSeal Matchroom League Results

S. Hendry 5, W. Thorne 3; N. Foulds 5, C. Thorburn 3; D. Mountjoy 5, A. Meo 3; Meo 5, Foulds 3; S. Davis 7, Thorne 1; Hendry 4, Dennis Taylor 4; Taylor 6, Meo 2; Hendry 6, Thorburn 2; J. White 4, Thorne 4; Thorburn 5, J. Parrott 3; Foulds 7, Parrott 1; Davis 4, White 4; Thorne 6, Meo 2; Thorne 4, Mountjoy 4; White 5, Parrott 3; Davis 6, Thorburn 2; Hendry 6, Foulds 2; Foulds 8, Taylor 0; Hendry 5, Mountjoy 3; Thorne 6, Thorburn 2; Parrott 4, Taylor 4; Davis 5, Mountjoy 3; Davis 5, Foulds 3; Parrott 5, Hendry 3; Thorne 5, Foulds 3; Davis 5, Meo 3; Meo 5, Thorburn 3; Davis 4, Parrott 4; Parrott 4, Thorne 4; Thorburn 7, White 1; Taylor 4, Mountjoy 4; White 4, Foulds 4; Mountjoy 5, White 3; Mountjoy 6, Foulds 2; Meo 5, Hendry 3; Mountjoy 5, Parrott 3; Davis 6, Taylor 2; White 5, Hendry 3; Taylor 6, White 2; Thorne 5, Taylor 3; Taylor 5, Thorburn 3; Thorburn 6, Mountjoy 2; White 4, Meo 4; Parrott 6, Meo 2; Hendry 6, Davis 2.

StormSeal Matchroom League: Final Table

	P	W	D	L	F	A	Pts	Prize Money (£)
Steve Davis (Eng)	9	6	2	1	44	28	20	70,000
Stephen Hendry (Scot)	9	5	1	3	41	31	16	30,000
Willie Thorne (Eng)	9	4	3	2	38	34	15	25,000
Doug Mountjoy (Wales)	9	4	2	3	37	35	14	20,000
Dennis Taylor (NI)	9	3	3	3	34	38	12	17,000
Neal Foulds (Eng)	9	3	1	5	37	35	10	15,000
Jimmy White (Eng)	9	2	4	3	32	40	10	13,000
Tony Meo (Eng)	9	3	1	5	31	41	10	11,000
Cliff Thorburn (Can)	9	3	0	6	33	39	9	9,000
John Parrott (Eng)	9	2	3	4	33	39	9	5,000

High break: 142 – John Parrott £5,000

Matchroom International League Results

J. White 5, S. Davis 3; A. Meo 5, Davis 3; Davis 4, A. Higgins 4; Meo 5, Higgins 3; T. Griffiths 7, Higgins 1; Davis 4, Griffiths 4; White 5, Higgins 3; White 6, Hallett 2; White 4, Griffiths 4; Davis 6, Hallett 2; Griffiths 6, Hallett 2; Meo 3, White 3; Griffiths 3, Meo 4; Meo 8, Hallett 0; Hallett 6, Higgins 2.

Matchroom International League: Final Table

	P	W	D	L	F	A	Pts	Prize Money (£)
Tony Meo (Eng)	5	4	1	0	27	13	13	25,000
Jimmy White (Eng)	5	3	1	1	23	17	10	12,000
Terry Griffiths (Wales)	5	2	3	0	25	15	9	10,000
Steve Davis (Eng)	5	1	2	2	20	20	5	8,000
Mike Hallett (Eng)	5	1	0	4	12	28	3	6,000
Alex Higgins (NI)	5	0	1	4	13	27	1	5,000

High break: 135 – Jimmy White £4,000

EMBASSY WORLD CHAMPIONSHIP

The Selly Park British Legion Club was the less-than-exotic venue when Alex 'Hurricane' Higgins became the youngest world champion at the age of twenty-two years and eleven months in 1972. That record stood for eighteen years until last season when Stephen Hendry, at twenty-one years and three months, lifted the Embassy World Championship trophy aloft after an 18–12 beating of Jimmy White in the more glamorous setting of the Crucible Theatre in Sheffield.

In 1986, sixteen-year-old Hendry had qualified for the first round proper at the Crucible but lost 10–8 to Willie Thorne. Even so, Hendry made a vow to return within five years and become the youngest world champion. He kept that promise in style and took the £120,000 first prize after a two-day high-speed potting battle that left the sell-out crowd virtually breathless.

White trailed 9–7 overnight and then found himself 13–7 behind as Hendry won four frames in magnificent style. Hendry said later: 'They are the best four frames I have ever played.' White staged a fightback, but after that opening burst there was only going to be one winner and Hendry finally clinched the title with a break of 81.

Hendry's victory also signalled a power shift in world snooker as he took the world number 1 position from deposed champion Steve Davis. It was the first time Davis had been off the number 1 position since 1983.

Well played, boyo!: Darren Morgan with a good luck message from Labour leader Neil Kinnock during the World Championship.

Embassy World Championship Results

FIRST ROUND		SECOND ROUND	QUARTER-FINALS	SEMI-FINALS	FINAL
S. Davis (Eng)	10				
v		S. Davis	13		
E. Charlton (Aust)	1				
		v	S. Davis	13	
S. James (Eng)	10				
v		James	7		
A. Higgins (NI)	5				
			v	S. Davis	14
W. Thorne (Eng)	10				
v		Thorne	11		
A. Drago (Malta)	4				
		v	N. Foulds	8	
Dennis Taylor (NI)	8				
v		N. Foulds	13		
N. Foulds (Eng)	10				
				v	White	12
T. Griffiths (Wales)	10				
v		Griffiths	13		
N. Gilbert (Eng)	4				
		v	Griffiths	5	
A. Knowles (Eng)	10				
v		Knowles	6		
A. Chappel (Wales)	4				
			v	White	16
J. Virgo (Eng)	10				
v		Virgo	6		
Gary Wilkinson (Eng)	6				
		v	White	13	
J. White (Eng)	10				
v		White	13		
D. Fowler (Eng)	4				v
S. Hendry (Scot)	10				
v		Hendry	13		
A. Robidoux (Can)	7				
		v	Hendry	13	
A. Meo (Eng)	10				
v		Meo	7		
W. Jones (Wales)	8				
			v	Hendry	16
J. Johnson (Eng)	8				
v		D. Morgan	13		
D. Morgan (Wales)	10				
		v	D. Morgan	6	
M. Hallett (Eng)	10				
v		Hallett	8		
S. Newbury (Wales)	9				
				v	Hendry	18
C. Thorburn (Can)	10				
v		Thorburn	13		
C. Wilson (Wales)	6				
		v	Thorburn	6	
D. Mountjoy (Wales)	10				
v		Mountjoy	12		
B. Gollan (Can)	8				
			v	Parrott	11
D. Reynolds (Eng)	10				
v		Reynolds	11		
P. Francisco (SA)	7				
		v	Parrott	13	
J. Parrott (Eng)	10				
v		Parrott	13		
M. Bennett (Wales)	9				

Losers: £5,000	Losers: £9,000	Losers: £18,000	Losers: £36,000	Loser: £72,000
				Winner: £120,000

High break: 140 – J. Parrott £12,000

'I would like to think I could dominate snooker just like Steve did in the 1980s. It would be nice to beat him at the Crucible, because after all that was Steve's domain in the last few years,' said the new world champion.

Davis had departed in the semi-final after a magnificent game with White which the 'Whirlwind' won 16–14. It was hailed as one of the greatest matches seen at the Crucible. In the other semi-final Hendry had a battle royal with John Parrott, the beaten finalist the year before. Parrott led 4–0, trailed 10–6, levelled at 11–11 and finally went down 16–11.

One of Hendry's toughest moments came in the first round when he beat Canadian Alain Robidoux 10–7 after a match that was filled with controversy. Robidoux, level at 7–7, looked poised to make it 8–7 only to be called for a 'push shot' by refereee John Street. Hendry seized the initiative by winning that frame and the next two to go through 10–7, though Robidoux was adamant: 'It was not a push shot.'

Darren Morgan, a Welshman from Hendry's Cuemasters stable, battled valiantly to reach the quarter-final after recovering from chicken pox on the eve of the championship. In the end he was beaten by Hendry 13–6. Neal Foulds, the former world number 3, showed that he is still a force to be reckoned with as he reached the quarter-final with victories over Dennis Taylor and Willie Thorne and regained his place in the top sixteen.

Hendry, though, was the number 1 attraction: the starlet of the 1980s who seems certain to be the star of the 1990s.

World Championship Roll of Honour 1927–89

YEAR	WINNER	RUNNER-UP	SCORE	VENUE
1927	J. Davis (Eng)	T. Dennis (Eng)	20–11	Camkin's Hall, Birmingham
1928	J. Davis (Eng)	F. Lawrence (Eng)	16–13	Camkin's Hall, Birmingham
1929	J. Davis (Eng)	T. Dennis (Eng)	19–14	Lounge Billiard Hall, Nottingham
1930	J. Davis (Eng)	T. Dennis (Eng)	25–12	Thurston's Hall, London
1931	J. Davis (Eng)	T. Dennis (Eng)	25–21	Lounge Billiard Hall, Nottingham
1932	J. Davis (Eng)	C. McConachy (NZ)	30–19	Thurston's Hall, London
1933	J. Davis (Eng)	W. Smith (Eng)	25–18	Joe Davis Billiards Centre, Chesterfield
1934	J. Davis (Eng)	T. Newman (Eng)	25–23	Lounge Billiard Hall, Nottingham
1935	J. Davis (Eng)	W. Smith (Eng)	25–20	Thurston's Hall, London
1936	J. Davis (Eng)	H. Lindrum (Aust)	34–27	Thurston's Hall, London
1937	J. Davis (Eng)	J. Lindrum (Aust)	32–29	Thurston's Hall, London
1938	J. Davis (Eng)	S. Smith (Eng)	37–24	Thurston's Hall, London
1939	J. Davis (Eng)	S. Smith (Eng)	43–30	Thurston's Hall, London
1940	J. Davis (Eng)	F. Davis (Eng)	37–36	Thurston's Hall, London
1941–45	No tournament held			
1946	J. Davis (Eng)	H. Lindrum (Aust)	78–67	Horticultural Hall, London
1947	W. Donaldson (Scot)	F. Davis (Eng)	82–63	Leicester Square Hall, London
1948	F. Davis (Eng)	W. Donaldson (Scot)	84–61	Leicester Square Hall, London
1949	F. Davis (Eng)	W. Donaldson (Scot)	80–65	Leicester Square Hall, London
1950	W. Donaldson (Scot)	F. Davis (Eng)	51–46	Tower Circus, Blackpool
1951	F. Davis (Eng)	W. Donaldson (Scot)	58–39	Tower Circus, Blackpool

BA&CC Tournament

YEAR	WINNER	RUNNER-UP	SCORE	VENUE
1952	H. Lindrum (Aust)	C. McConachy (NZ)	94–49	Houldsworth Hall, Manchester

World Matchplay Championship

YEAR	WINNER	RUNNER-UP	SCORE
1952	F. Davis (Eng)	W. Donaldson (Scot)	38–35
1953	F. Davis (Eng)	W. Donaldson (Scot)	37–34
1954	F. Davis (Eng)	W. Donaldson (Scot)	39–21
1955	F. Davis (Eng)	J. Pulman (Eng)	37–34
1956	F. Davis (Eng)	J. Pulman (Eng)	38–35
1957	J. Pulman (Eng)	J. Rea (NI)	39–34

Between 1958 and 1963 no matches took place. From 1964 the title was decided on a challenge basis which meant that there was often more than one event per year.

YEAR	WINNER	RUNNER-UP	SCORE	VENUE
1964	J. Pulman (Eng)	F. Davis (Eng)	19–16	Burroughes Hall, London
	J. Pulman (Eng)	R. Williams (Eng)	40–33	Burroughes Hall, London
1965	J. Pulman (Eng)	F. Davis (Eng)	37–36	Burroughes Hall, London
	J. Pulman (Eng)	R. Williams (Eng)	25–22	Match series in South Africa
	J. Pulman (Eng)	F. van Rensburg (SA)	39–12	South Africa
1966	J. Pulman (Eng)	F. Davis (Eng)	5–2	Match series at St George's Hall, Liverpool
1967	No tournament held			
1968	J. Pulman (Eng)	E. Charlton (Aus)	39–34	Co-operative Hall, Bolton
1969	Championship again organised on a knock-out basis (Players No. 6)			
	J. Spencer (Eng) (Players No. 6)	G. Owen (Wales)	37–24	Victoria Hall, London
1970	R. Reardon (Wales) (actually held Nov 1970 as a round robin)	J. Pulman (Eng)	37–33	Victoria Hall, London
1971	J. Spencer (Eng) (reverted to knockout basis)	W. Simpson (Aust)	37–29	Sydney, Australia
1972	A. Higgins (NI) (Park Drive)	J. Spencer (Eng)	37–32	Selly Park British Legion, Birmingham
1973	R. Reardon (Wales) (Park Drive)	E. Charlton (Aus)	38–32	City Exhibition Hall, Manchester
1974	R. Reardon (Wales)	G. Miles (Eng)	22–12	Belle Vue, Manchester
1975	R. Reardon (Wales) (Embassy until present day)	E. Charlton	31–30	Melbourne, Australia
1976	R. Reardon (Wales)	A. Higgins (NI)	27–16	Town Hall, Middlesbrough, and Wythenshawe Forum, Manchester
1977	J. Spencer (Eng)	C. Thorburn (Can)	25–12	Crucible Theatre, Sheffield
1978	R. Reardon (Wales)	P. Mans (SA)	25–18	Crucible Theatre, Sheffield
1979	T. Griffiths (Wales)	Dennis Taylor (NI)	24–16	Crucible Theatre, Sheffield
1980	C. Thorburn (Can)	A. Higgins (NI)	18–16	Crucible Theatre, Sheffield
1981	S. Davis (Eng)	D. Mountjoy (Wales)	18–12	Crucible Theatre, Sheffield
1982	A. Higgins (NI)	R. Reardon (Wales)	18–15	Crucible Theatre, Sheffield
1983	S. Davis (Eng)	C. Thorburn (Can)	18–6	Crucible Theatre, Sheffield
1984	S. Davis (Eng)	J. White (Eng)	18–16	Crucible Theatre, Sheffield
1985	Dennis Taylor (NI)	S. Davis (Eng)	18–17	Crucible Theatre, Sheffield
1986	J. Johnson (Eng)	S. Davis (Eng)	18–12	Crucible Theatre, Sheffield
1987	S. Davis (Eng)	J. Johnson (Eng)	18–14	Crucible Theatre, Sheffield
1988	S. Davis (Eng)	T. Griffiths (Wales)	18–11	Crucible Theatre, Sheffield
1989	S. Davis (Eng)	J. Parrott (Eng)	18–3	Crucible Theatre, Sheffield

SATELLITE TOURNAMENTS

The WPBSA initiated additional events for players who were knocked out in the early stages of certain ranking tournaments. Two of these satellite tournaments were held last season – the Favorite Fried Chicken Satellite Tournament in Clacton, Essex, and the Professional Players Satellite Tournament in Glasgow.

FAVORITE FRIED CHICKEN SATELLITE TOURNAMENT

Rob Foldvari, who once took the world professional billiards title, earned £5,000 after winning his first professional snooker title in the Favorite Fried Chicken Satellite Tournament which was held in Clacton, Essex. Using a brand-new cue, he hammered Welshman Darren Morgan 8–1 in the final with an incredible string of breaks of 98, 76, 65, 42 and 80 – and all that after Morgan had won the first frame. Foldvari had been suffering with a painful shoulder problem and he said: 'When I was back in Australia, I went to see a Chinese doctor who gave me a load of pills to take. I had to take six a day for three weeks, but they seemed to work.'

Favorite Fried Chicken Satellite Tournament Results

QUARTER-FINALS:	R. Foldvari (Aust) bt A. Chappel (Wales) 5–3; David Taylor (Eng) bt A. Drago (Malta) 5–2; D. Morgan (Wales) bt John Rea (Scot) 5–1; M. Bennett (Wales) bt D. Fowler (Eng) 5–2
	Losers: £600
SEMI-FINALS:	Foldvari bt David Taylor 5–3; D. Morgan bt Bennett 5–1
	Losers: £1,200
FINAL:	Foldvari bt D. Morgan 8–1
	Loser: £2,500
	Winner: £5,000

High break: 140 – A. Drago £500

PROFESSIONAL PLAYERS SATELLITE TOURNAMENT

Ken Owers, who started last season at number 75 in the rankings, picked up £5,000 with his first title on the professional circuit in the Professional Players Satellite Tournament in Glasgow. A professional since 1986, Owers included a break of 107 in his 9–6 defeat of Hornchurch's Dave Gilbert.

Irishman Steve Murphy, a first-year professional, included three centuries of 120, 111 and 102 in a 5–2 second-round defeat of Tommy Murphy. Steve, from Dublin, looked certain to score a 147 after knocking in fifteen reds and fifteen blacks but then, using the rest, failed on what seemed an easy yellow with a break of 120.

Professional Players Satellite Tournament Results

QUARTER-FINALS:	K. Owers (Eng) bt N. Bond (Eng) 5–3; A. Cairns (Eng) bt M. Price (Eng) 5–3; D. Gilbert (Eng) bt J. McLaughlin (NI) 5–3; A. Chappel (Wales) bt S. Newbury (Wales) 5–0
	Losers: £600
SEMI-FINALS:	Owers bt Cairns 6–4; D. Gilbert bt Chappel 6–3
	Losers: £1,200
FINAL:	Owers bt D. Gilbert 9–6
	Loser: £2,500
	Winner: £5,000

High break: 126 – C. Edwards £450

NATIONAL CHAMPIONSHIPS

Last season the WPBSA, in an economy drive, decided to cut the £1,000 per man subsidy for the National Championships. This meant that no national tournaments were held unless they were independently sponsored. The result was that only one national championship continued in the 1989/90 season – the Welsh tournament, which was sponsored, as in the 1988/89 season, by Senator Windows.

SENATOR WINDOWS WELSH CHAMPIONSHIP

Darren Morgan, who had taken the Welsh amateur title in 1987, added the Welsh professional crown to his list of honours when he beat defending champion Doug Mountjoy 9–7 in the final of the Senator Windows Welsh Championship in Newport. The man from Cwmfelinfach earned £10,500 plus a £1,200 bonus for the high break of 130 which he knocked in during the final. It was also the highest break recorded in the history of the tournament.

Morgan, a former world amateur champion, trailed 4–3 at the end of the afternoon session, but then started the evening with that break of 130 and moved into a 7–4 lead. Mountjoy reduced the deficit to 7–6, then the next two frames were shared before Morgan compiled an excellent 80 to clinch the title.

Yet Morgan could have gone out in the first round when he trailed Colin Roscoe 4–3, but he recovered to go through 6–4.

Welsh wizard: Darren Morgan (centre) picks up his trophy from BBC commentator Ted Lowe (right) and David Jenkins of Senator Windows after his victory in the Senator Windows Welsh Championship.

He beat Terry Griffiths 6–4 in the quarter-final and then had to take the final two frames to beat Tony Chappel 9–8. Mountjoy disposed of Ray Reardon 6–3 in the quarter-final and then knocked out Wayne Jones 9–7, but there was to be no title repeat as Morgan deservedly won his first major professional tournament.

Senator Windows Welsh Championship Results

FIRST ROUND		QUARTER-FINALS		SEMI-FINALS		FINAL	
		D. Mountjoy	6				
M. Bennett	2	v		Mountjoy	9		
v		Reardon	3				
R. Reardon	6			v		Mountjoy	7
		S. Newbury	3				
		v		W. Jones	7		
		W. Jones	6				
						v	
		C. Wilson	4				
		v		Chappel	8		
		A. Chappel	6				
C. Roscoe	4			v		D. Morgan	9
v		D. Morgan	6				
D. Morgan	6	v		D. Morgan	9		
		T. Griffiths	4				
Losers: £500		Losers: £900		Losers: £2,750		Loser: £6,000	
						Winner: £10,500	

High break: 130 – D. Morgan £1,200

OTHER TOURNAMENTS

BRITISH CAR RENTAL WORLD CUP

England, represented by Steve Davis, John Parrott and Jimmy White, went into the British Car Rental World Cup at the Bournemouth International Centre as the bookmakers' favourite to win the title for the third year running. Four days later the England trio were already back at home when the happy-go-lucky Canadians lifted the trophy for the second time, having beaten Northern Ireland 9–5 to pick up the £48,000 winners' cheque.

Over the years the Canadians have always been renowned for their team spirit, though skipper Cliff Thorburn was the only survivor from the side that won the World Cup for the first time in 1982. Last season he was joined by Alain Robidoux and Bob Chaperon, who had just been crowned British Open champion.

Canada's undoubted hero was Robidoux, who won ten of his twelve frames, including five out of the six in the final. Bournemouth snooker fans have always responded well to this event and the sell-out crowd was treated to a memorable final when Robidoux scored a 124 in the final frame to clinch the title and give his team a £6,000 high break bonus.

The World Cup offers a different format for the snooker follower, with short sharp matches the order of the day. Certainly England's involvement was short and sharp as they were beaten 5–4 by the under-rated Republic of Ireland side in the quarter-final. The Republic were 4–1 down, but in the end it was Dubliner Paddy Browne who beat Davis in the decider 68–28. It was the first time Browne had ever played against Davis in competition.

Off the table, Northern Ireland team-mates Alex Higgins and Dennis Taylor were involved in a long and bitter verbal dispute and that hardly helped morale in the final. In the semi-finals Northern Ireland had beaten the Republic of Ireland 5–2 after the first ever snooker meeting between the two countries, while Canada had seen off Australia 5–1.

The Canadians, who had spent their days off playing golf together, certainly

Canadian crackers: The Canadian trio of (left to right) Alain Robidoux, Cliff Thorburn and Bob Chaperon after their triumph in the British Car Rental World Cup.

enjoyed the celebrations. Team member Robidoux declared: 'This is the greatest moment of my life.'

British Car Rental World Cup Results

	QUARTER-FINALS		SEMI-FINALS		FINAL	
S. Davis J. Parrott J. White	England	4				
	v		Republic of Ireland	2		
E. Hughes P. Browne A. Kearney	Republic of Ireland	5				
			v		Northern Ireland	5
Dennis Taylor A. Higgins T. Murphy	Northern Ireland	5				
	v		Northern Ireland	5		
S. Francisco (SA) D. O'Kane (NZ) A. Drago (Malta)	Rest of the World	2			v	
C. Thorburn R. Chaperon A. Robidoux	Canada	5				
	v		Canada	5		
S. Hendry M. Macleod John Rea	Scotland	3				
			v		Canada	9
E. Charlton J. Campbell W. King	Australia	5				
	v		Australia	1		
T. Griffiths D. Mountjoy C. Wilson	Wales	3				
	Losers: £9,000		Losers: £15,000		Losers: £30,000 Winners: £48,000	

High break: 124 – A. Robidoux £6,000 (shared by the team)

Previous Years' Results

YEAR	WINNER	RUNNER-UP	SCORE
1979	(State Express) Wales	England	14–3
1980	(State Express) Wales	Canada	8–5
1981	(State Express) England	Wales	4–3
1982	(State Express) Canada	England	4–2
1983	(State Express) England	Wales	4–2
1985	(Guinness) Ireland A	England A	9–7
1986	(Car Care) Ireland A	Canada	9–7
1987	(Tuborg) Ireland A	Canada	9–2
1988	(Fersina) England	Australia	9–7
1989	(Fersina) England	Rest of the World	9–8

NORWICH UNION EUROPEAN GRAND PRIX

Monte Carlo is a principality that plays host to millionaires, playboys, film stars, budding actresses and many of the world's top sporting tax exiles. Joe Johnson does not fit any of these categories, but he certainly enjoyed his brief stop-over in Monaco for the final stages of the Norwich Union European Grand Prix. His last tournament win had been the Langs Supreme Scottish Masters in 1987 and he was not the favourite to win the £20,000 first prize, yet that did not stop him beating Stephen Hendry 5–3 in the final. Johnson said: 'It wasn't much of a match, but I am delighted.'

Hendry had looked much sharper in his semi-final when breaks of 59, 46, 49 and 112 gave him a 4–0 success over Tony Knowles, while Johnson squeezed past John Parrott by a 4–3 margin.

Norwich Union European Grand Prix Results

QUARTER-FINALS: J. Parrott (Eng) bt M. Hallett (Eng) 5–4; J. Johnson (Eng) bt D. Mountjoy (Wales) 5–4; A. Knowles (Eng) bt M. Clark (Eng) 5–3; S. Hendry (Scot) bt J. Virgo (Eng) 5–0
Losers: £2,500

SEMI-FINALS: Johnson bt Parrott 4–3; Hendry bt Knowles 4–0
Losers: £5,000

FINAL: Johnson bt Hendry 5–3
Loser: £10,000
Winner: £20,000

High break: 137 – Mike Hallett Weekend in Monte Carlo

Previous Years' Results

YEAR	WINNER	RUNNER-UP	SCORE
1988	S. Davis (Eng)	J. White (Eng)	5–4

WHO SAID THAT?

'Cutting out the Inderal beta-blocker meant I could apply to become a professional snooker player again. I was getting depressed because my snooker cue was in mothballs.'

– Bill Werbeniuk talking about his decision to stop taking the banned drug Inderal and being allowed back into the professional ranks.

'This is war between Matchroom and Cuemasters, England and Scotland. The Scots have come over Hadrian's Wall and pillaged our trophies. We won't tolerate it.'

– Matchroom chairman Barry Hearn after Stephen Hendry, the Cuemasters number 1, had won the Embassy world title.

'My brain cells will do headstands if I go on to win this title.'

– Alex Higgins after beating Steve James 9–3 in the semi-final of the Pearl Assurance British Open.

'I have lost all my respect for Davis and I used to idolise him. I just think it was an old pro trick.'

– Craig Edwards after a dispute in the European Open when opponent Steve Davis asked the referee if Edwards had played a 'push shot'.

'Craig was upset? I had steam coming out of my ears after a shot which I thought was a push shot had left me on the bottom rail.'

– Steve Davis commenting on the criticisms by Craig Edwards during the European Open.

The power game: Barry Hearn (left) of Matchroom and Ian Doyle of Cuemasters, the two most powerful managers in snooker, during one of their less war-like moments.

'I was shell-shocked and dazed. I got worse and worse and he got better and better.'

— *Jimmy White after losing 9–0 to Gary Wilkinson in the quarter-final of the StormSeal UK Open.*

'I never even thought to look at the scoreboard because I thought Davis had only needed the one snooker.'

— *Gary Wilkinson after adding up the scores wrongly in his semi-final with Steve Davis in the StormSeal UK Open which Davis went on to win 9–8.*

'The association doesn't allow you to take pills.'

— *Alex Higgins after winning his semi-final in the Pearl Assurance British Open and being offered a bottle of Pils lager.*

'My wife likes the beard, but my manager Ian Doyle says I look like Genghis Khan.'

— *Joe Johnson (above), the former world champion, discussing his new-look beard.*

THE SHOT OF THE SEASON

No doubt about this one as Robert Marshall comes off four cushions to strike the yellow after being snookered by Steve Newbury in the quarter-final of the Pearl Assurance British Open at Derby. Marshall went on to win 5–4 before going down 9–5 to Bob Chaperon, the eventual winner, in the semi-final.

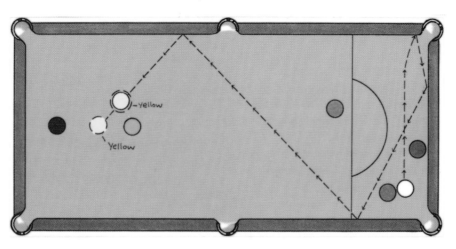

EARTHQUAKES ON THURSDAY ISLAND AND BILLIARDS IN A LIONS' DEN!

by Roger Lee

Professional snooker is a multi-million pound sporting industry. The top players are very rich, sponsors pour in fortunes and what started as a sport for relaxation has turned into a test of nerves. Thankfully, however, snooker and billiards can be fun. The sports have enjoyed a chequered history and there have been moments in years gone by when humour has ruled the day. Let's wander through time and look at some of the lighter moments.

Billiards was 'invented' in the middle of the sixteenth century by William Kew, a London pawnbroker who, during wet weather, was in the habit of taking down the three balls that formed the traditional sign outside his shop and pushing them around his counter with the 'yard' stick. It became a great amusement for the young clergymen from nearby St Paul's Cathedral, hence the adoption in the game of the term 'cannon'. The game was then known by the name 'Billyard' because it was Bill (William) who first played with his 'yard' measure, while the word 'cue' came from William Kew's surname.

That sounds a reasonable explanation and the same can be said for the 'story' behind the invention of snooker. This, according to some people, was first played by a Captain Snooker, who was an officer in the Bengal Artillery and played his game throughout India during the 1870s. Now, the name 'Snook' is quite common, as any phone directory will show, but 'Snooker'? That is unusual.

It was Herbert Spencer who reputedly provided us with the quote 'Proficiency at billiards is the sign of a mis-spent youth'; while Edward VII's 'No gentleman ever made a break of more than 25' gives us the impression that our game was not held in too high esteem in the good old days. The following stories did nothing to improve that image.

The American novelist Mark Twain was a very keen and useful billiards player and was once asked to give a speech at the opening of a billiards tournament in New York. He chose billiards as his topic and began by stating that the game had destroyed his naturally sweet disposition.

'Once, when I was an underpaid reporter

It were not best that we should all think alike; it is difference of opinion that makes horse-races.

Mark Twain

Billiards fan: American novelist Mark Twain (right).

in Virginia City,' he said, 'a stranger came to town and opened a billiards parlour. I went to see him and he proposed a game, to which I agreed. "Before we begin," he said, "knock the balls around a little so that I can assess if any handicapping is required."

'I did so for a while and then he said: "I'll be perfectly fair with you: I will play you left-handed." I felt hurt at this, for he was cross-eyed, freckled and had red hair, so I was determined to teach him a lesson for his audacity. But he won the toss, got in first, and continued to play the game out, after which he took my half-dollar, and all I got was the opportunity to chalk my cue. "If you play like that with your left hand," I said, "I'd like to see you play with your right." "I can't," was the prompt reply, "I'm left-handed!" '

And so we continue. An artful thief, who was accompanied by several confederates, induced a trustful elderly gentleman for a wager to try to balance a billiard ball on his wrinkled brow for three minutes. While the old gentleman was bending back, keeping as still as possible, he was quietly relieved of his watch, chain and wallet. The thieves disappeared, leaving the gentleman and billiard ball perfectly balanced – something his cash wasn't when the three minutes were up.

Another tale concerns a few friends who were having a four-handed game of snooker. Just as they had finished, a young man entered the room and challenged any one of them to a game, an offer which was taken up by the group's best player. The stranger then asked if they would like a bit of 'interest' on the game, which was

'**The first billiards tournament**': a humorous portrayal by an early twentieth-century magazine devoted to the game.

Billiards in the tropics: An early picture.

agreed, and several pounds were imprudently left, for the time being, in the hands of the stranger. He proceeded to break the pack, after which he took his jacket off, hung it up and asked for the whereabouts of the toilet. Informed of this, he went out and was never seen again, leaving the group the poorer of their stakes except for an old worthless jacket with nothing in its pockets.

Over the years the professional billiards and snooker player has been asked to work in some wonderful and strange locations. Here are some venues which might put the best of us off our shot.

George Nelson, who was a well-known professional player and table manufacturer of the early part of this century, was asked to play an exhibition at a Yorkshire asylum (today's psychiatric hospital) which had 2,000 patients and housed twelve billiard tables. When it was not his turn to play, he dropped into the nearest available chair, next to a fat amiable-looking patient. After doing this several times, he then sat next to one of the chief warders, who said to

The greatest billiards player of all time: Walter Lindrum.

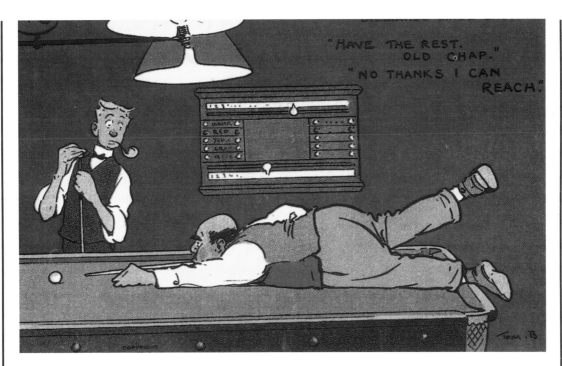

him: 'You see my ear?' Nelson looked at the organ indicated, out of which a good-sized piece was clearly missing. 'Well,' continued the warder, 'that chap you keep sitting next to bit that out.' Nelson thanked him and proceeded to concentrate more on his sitting position rather than his game from then on.

Melbourne Inman, who was a champion billiards player during the early part of this century, once played on Thursday Island in the Pacific Ocean. When he arrived, he found the shore full of wreckage. Inquiring the reason for the damage, he was informed that they had just had an earthquake on the island.

'Do you have them often?' asked Inman.

'Oh yes, quite often,' was the reply as two coffins were being carried past. He was also informed that the lighthouse on the island hadn't been seen since the previous earthquake, and for the same reason the billiard table was out of level. Inman duly fulfilled his engagement, but was first on the ship the following day.

In those early times playing in tropical regions presented problems which for-tunately are not experienced today at the Crucible Theatre in Sheffield.

A report from tropical Beira at the turn of this century summed up how difficult it was to get through a game without being interrupted. It read:

If you are enjoying a temporary respite from the ever-present malaria yourself, it is almost certain that your opponent, or someone else in the room, will be suffering from it, and be taken with the shakes, and this sort of thing puts a man off terribly. On the seats are men of all shades of hue. Years ago they were white, but yellow fever, jaundice and malaria have wiped out their original colour. Then someone gets a chill and the victim stuffs a quantity of quinine down his throat or calls loudly for whisky. The climate of Beira destroys everything: even the tables deteriorate, and are not true after they have been set up for a year or so. At closing time the customers are seen running down the street at top speed. This is done not to avoid paying for the time at the table, but to escape from the miasma which arrives from the marshy land at night, and which is laden with fever germs. As a consequence, first-class billiards or snooker is the exception rather than the rule.

A billiards match has also been played in a lions' den. This took place in England at Stoke-on-Trent in 1906, and everything was OK until one of the players dropped his cue, which startled the lions into running around the cage. The 2,000 audience was thus inspired with everything but confidence and several women fainted.

They say ignorance is bliss – well, it also makes for some good stories. These often occur when an uninitiated spectator is watching a professional at work, not really understanding what is going on. A good example was when Walter Lindrum, the greatest player of English billiards of all time, was making one of his big breaks, and was occupying the table for two or three sessions at a time. A stranger wandered into Thurston's Matchroom in Leicester Square and, after watching Lindrum for some considerable period, he turned to the doorman and said: 'What is the game he is playing?'

'Billiards, sir,' came the reply.

'Oh, they play with two players where I come from,' said the stranger, 'but I suppose it's different in London.'

Club officials also have their moments of mirth. For example, the chairman of a little club in Lancashire had been on his holidays, and during his absence the committee had the cloth of the snooker table shifted round with a new baulk line and D marked at the other end. On his return the chairman went into the snooker room and looked with admiration at the table, expressing pleasure at the improvement, concluding with the remark: 'But I cannot understand how you managed to turn such a big heavy table around in such a small room as this.'

Then there was the case of two professionals who were playing a match at a club near Leeds. After a while they both noticed how strangely the balls were running and, despite a close inspection, were uncertain of the all-important factor of which way the nap of the cloth was lying. At half-time, therefore, they asked who had ironed the table, and the steward's wife said that she had. On further inquiry as to which way it had been ironed, the good lady replied: 'Ah! I forgot which way it had to be ironed, so I ironed it both ways to be sure.'

At a team match between two village clubs in Lancashire, one player from the club which did not possess a rest climbed on to the table to make a stroke. The referee called: 'Foul.'

'What for?' asked the player.

The referee replied: 'For having both feet off the floor whilst making your shot.'

'That's funny,' answered the player. 'At our club you're all right if you keep one foot in the D.'

Great rivals: Melbourne Inman (left) and Tom Reece at Thurston's, Leicester Square, in 1935.

It's not only players who do not always know the rules. During a billiards tournament between two great players of the Edwardian period, Charles Dawson and Fred Bateman, the official referee failed to turn up. A volunteer more familiar with boxing than with billiards stepped in. He smoked a pipe throughout the session, and Dawson, who was playing intricate close cannons, stopped and asked him if the balls were touching. In bending down to observe the situation, the referee allowed the ash from his pipe to fall on to the table immediately where the three balls laid. He simply picked the balls up, blew away the ash, replaced the balls in a heap and declared: 'Not touching.'

In another match Tom Reece was making a fairly big break and had to play a tricky shot with his left hand. A gentleman in the front row of seats said to the lady by his side: 'Amphibious my dear, amphibious.'

Tom Reece was used to this kind of banter, as he had a great rival in Melbourne Inman, and any match between these two usually resulted in a war of words at some stage. In one such meeting Inman was fluking in a manner which made Reece's hair stand on end. At last the latter jumped up and asked with solemnity: 'How did you get that shot, Mr Inman?'

There was a momentary pause and then Inman replied: 'I believe you know my terms for tuition, Mr Reece.'

Reece and Inman were asked to give an exhibition at Buckingham Palace before the King, and just before entering the billiard room Inman advised Reece to play an open game as His Majesty was not keen on watching the close cannon game for which Reece was famous. Reece duly obliged and was beaten easily by Inman who 'ran out' the match with a run of close cannons.

'I thought you said the King didn't like to watch close cannon play,' said Reece later.

Pay rise? Are you sure?: John Spencer, three times world champion.

'Didn't you notice the dark look he gave me?' replied the smiling Inman.

During the mid-1970s I used to book John Spencer to play exhibitions in the Norfolk area, and his fee was £90 per evening. He then returned in 1978 and did a marvellous night at a club in Norwich, making three centuries plus many breaks over 50, and everyone was delighted. So much so that, at the end of the evening, the club's chairman pressed an extra tenner in my hand.

Outside in the car park I congratulated John on a great night, and said: 'They were so pleased John, they increased your fee from £90 to £100.'

'That's great,' answered Spencer, 'except that this year my exhibition fee has gone up to £140.'

Well, he had just won the World Championship!

Clip joint: Tony Drago enjoys a short back and smiles after visiting the local hairdressers during the Mercantile Credit Classic in Blackpool.

Eyes down: Tony Knowles caught in a quite unflattering pose by our cameraman.

Spot the Leo!: Steve Davis, born under the sign of Leo, and a cuddly friend who was donated to charity during the StormSeal UK Open.

Spot the difference: John Spencer, the chairman of the WPBSA, and his double, Jim Elkins, the Tournament Director of Benson and Hedges. John is the one on the right — or it could be the left!

Cold comfort: Alan Green, the snooker commentator for BBC Radio 2, had to keep warm during a particularly cold day at the StormSeal UK Open in Preston last season. Believe it or not, he was *inside* the building at the time.

FUNNY GAME

Sleepy street: Referee John Street sports a natty hat after nodding off to sleep during a quiet moment at the Dubai Duty Free Classic.

Bathing beauties or beasts?: The referees (left to right) Alan Chamberlain, John Street, John Williams, Vic Bartlam and Len Ganley take it easy at the rooftop swimming pool during the Hong Kong Open.

Who's your friend?: Alex Higgins with his lucky leprechaun, which he called Antrim, during the Pearl Assurance British Open in Derby.

What a monster!: Cliff Wilson with a fish that was caught during a day at sea during the Dubai Duty Free Classic.

THE MAN BEHIND THE MIC: 'WHISPERING' TED LOWE

by Bruce Beckett

You don't often see the face but the voice is unmistakeable: 'And for those of you watching in black and white, the blue ball is behind the yellow.' It could only be the Voice of Snooker, 'Whispering' Ted Lowe. Ted, now in his thirty-sixth year as BBC Television's senior snooker commentator, has become a household sound – if not a name. Yet while his breeding always suggested a sporting life, the horse-racing industry seemed favourite from the off.

Edwin Charles Lowe was born into a racing family on 1 November 1920 and brought up in Lambourn, Berkshire. His father Ernest was travelling head lad to Oswald Bell, a leading trainer of the time. Among the owners Bell trained for was Sir Cunliffe-Owen, whose Felstead won the Epsom Derby in 1928. 'My first memory is of my father leading the horse back into the village,' says Ted. 'And in my youth I used to imagine I was one of the top jockeys – Gordon Richards, Harry Wragg or Brownie Carslake. It was my job to keep the copper pot containing linseed for the horses boiling.'

But Ted, one of four children, was never cut out for the turf. 'My father always said I would be too heavy to become a jockey and he was right.'

For a small village, Lambourn was well endowed with public houses. One of them, the Lamb, had been in the Lowe family for 300 years. Aunt Rose and Uncle Jim were the tenants and, as fate would have it, there was a small billiards table in the pub. At the age of seven 'Teddy' was discovering the delights of the green baize. 'Nobody else in the family played billiards. It was all horses. But I took to this and I couldn't

keep away from it. It wasn't very long before I was making 100 breaks,' he remembers.

Though no dunce at the village school, Ted was soon learning about the licensing trade. By the age of eleven he was pulling pints in the pub and proving a liquid asset to his aunt and uncle. Another uncle, Fred, also ran a pub – the Pied Bull in Streatham, London – and it was decided that Ted, now thirteen and a half, should go to the smoke. Imagine his joy when he found the pub contained a full-sized billiards table. 'That's where I learned to play snooker and it wasn't long before I was teaching the regulars how to play,' he recalls. 'My handicap was that I could only play the black ball, which taught me a lot about positioning.'

The only thing Ted didn't have was friends. So on his one afternoon off each week he took a bus to Thurston's – the home of snooker – in Leicester Square. 'I went to watch the greats play – Joe Davis ("The Sultan of Snooker"), Tom Newman, Willie Smith, Walter Lindrum, Claude

---

WHO SAID THAT?

'When I turned professional in 1946 Ted had just become the manager of Leicester Square Hall. Ted is known to millions throughout the world. His voice is unique. He is to snooker what John Arlott was to cricket.
'I was with Ted one day at Chester races when we bumped into Nick Hunter. It was that chance meeting that indirectly led to the BBC covering the World Championship.'

▲

– John Pulman.

Falkiner – names that were really magical in the world of billiards and snooker. It was there that I learned all sorts of things about the game, shots I would then try out in practice.'

Ted never made a century break at snooker but he was good enough to beat the English amateur champion, Percy Bendon, in a best-of-three-frames challenge match set up by his uncle. It wasn't until after the match, though, that he learned the identity of his opponent!

In between serving at the bar, Ted would mark in the billiards room. Not surprisingly, be became good with numbers and it was that talent that led to his next job. The Smith brothers, who frequented the pub, offered him the job of estimating and rate fixing with their company, Smith Meters, and much to his uncle's disgust he accepted. He started on a salary of 27 shillings (£1.35) a week, but it wasn't long before the outbreak of the Second World War. Ted volunteered for the Royal Air Force; he failed the medical,

> ### WHO SAID THAT?
>
> 'Ted is a great character and personality. He has never lost his love or interest in snooker and is always looking to see where he can help the game.
> 'He was largely responsible for talking the BBC into doing *Pot Black*. "Whispering" Ted Lowe has become the Voice of Snooker, what Henry Longhurst was to golf and Peter O'Sullevan is to horse-racing. Ted has always had a soft spot for the players left from the days of Leicester Square Hall.'
>
> ▲
>
> – *Rex Williams.*

however, and was assigned to munitions.

Snooker was never far from his mind and it was Ted who persuaded the Smiths to open a social club – the Meters Rifle and Social Club – and put a billiards table in one of the two Nissen huts erected at the back of the factory. Always an innovator, Ted then wrote to Joe Davis asking him if he would open the club. With the great

The greatest: Joe Davis (left) with Ted Lowe.

Official seal of approval: Top referees (left to right) John Smyth, John Williams, Len Ganley, Alan Chamberlain and John Street join in the fun at the launch of Ted Lowe's book, *Snooker Characters*. Also in the picture is caricaturist John Ireland.

man's appearance secured, Ted then wired Horace Lindrum – on his way to England from Australia by boat – to ask him if he was prepared to play Joe in an exhibition. It was quite a *coup* at the time as Lindrum was making his first visit to England. Seating for 530 was installed, but, says Ted, 'The world and his wife were after me to get tickets.' It was his idea to have an interval – something unheard of before.

While the company directors entertained the two players in the boardroom, he provided light refreshment and music for the spectators.

Much to Ted's horror, it had been arranged that he should play Joe in a one-frame challenge match. Joe gave him six blacks start and, despite shaking like a leaf, Ted potted the last red and all the colours to win by a point. 'Local Boy Makes Good' was the headline in the local paper.

The billiard table had been installed by W. Jelks and one of their directors was so impressed by Ted's initiative and organisational ability that he offered him a new job.

'He told me the company was planning to reopen Leicester Square Hall and that they wanted someone to run it,' says Ted. 'As you can imagine, I jumped at the

---

WHO SAID THAT?

'I have known Ted from the days of *Pot Black*. As well as bringing a lot to snooker commentary, he has helped sell and promote the game. One of my best memories of Ted is sharing a Kentucky Fried Chicken dinner with him in a hotel in Sydney at 4am!'

▲

– *Dennis Taylor.*

chance. Life for me changed from that moment on.

'My initiation into the world of professional billiards and snooker was with Jelks and the World Snooker Championship final of 1946, when Joe Davis beat Horace Lindrum at the Horticultural Hall in Westminster, London, to stay undefeated for twenty years, after which he retired from championship play. I helped behind the scenes.'

Leicester Square Hall, developed on the bombed-out site of Thurston's, became the world Mecca for professional billiards and snooker. 'I was head cook and bottle washer,' explains Ted. 'I ran the business side of things and prepared the agreements the players had to sign. There were no fees. They were all on percentages of the gate according to their status in the game. Joe Davis, being the top man, got a higher percentage than anyone else.'

Ted also set new standards, insisting that the players wore dark suits in the afternoon and evening dress at night. The Hall was open for forty-two weeks of the year. He also helped Joe Davis form the Professional Billiard Players Association, and there is no hiding his admiration for the man. 'Joe was *the* person in every way, shape and form. He became a second father to me. We worked very closely together for thirty-odd years.

'He was a marvellous man in so many ways. I admired his dress, I admired the way he worked, I admired his professionalism. He was full of ideas; he was an extraordinary person and, at the same time, he had this fabulous ability of artistry on the table. He had so many things. He really was an outstanding man.'

Ted, twenty-six when he went to Leicester Square Hall, was well aware of the need for publicity.

He used to phone the results of billiards and snooker matches through to the

What a trio: Ted Lowe (left) with Thelma Carpenter, a former women's professional billiards and snooker champion, and John Spencer, a former world champion and chairman of the WPBSA.

The Mecca of billiards and snooker: Leicester Square Hall after it was completely rebuilt. Ted Lowe was the manager.

media, and when rare broadcasts were made from Leicester Square Hall, Ted would assist with information. Raymond Glendenning was the top sports commentator of the day.

'I used to sit next to him and hand him bits of paper with the scores because he didn't know much about the game,' Ted says. 'In 1954 he came along to do a broadcast and he had lost his voice. I was thrown in at the deep end. They told me to get on and do it. You can imagine how scared I was. There was no commentary box. You sat in among the audience with people either side of you who had paid money to watch the stars play.

'Joe Davis was playing and, as director of Leicester Square Hall, I had always addressed him as "Sir". I now had to say, "Joe is going for this and Joe is going for that," which was one of the most difficult things I have ever had to do. I actually had to criticise his game if he did something wrong.

'I was so near the table I was in the first row with the audience either side of me and Joe was no more than 2 yards away. So I spoke very quietly – hence the whispering voice was born! It was printed in the press afterwards and has stuck with me ever since.'

One newspaper later wrote that Ted's voice sounded 'like a spider crawling over sand paper', but he explains: 'I have always looked upon the game of snooker as being played in a cathedral-like atmosphere and I have been told so many times that my voice, which is very quiet anyway, knits in well with the atmosphere that I now believe it must be true.'

The closure of Leicester Square Hall in January 1955 led to the temporary demise of professional snooker. It took away the game's shop window and left Ted without a job. The World Championship was staged elsewhere for the next two years but died completely in 1957. There was insufficient money to stage the championship and it was not played again until 1964.

Ted, thanks to his many contacts, had several job offers. He nearly signed for the *News of the World* but ended up 'back with the booze', joining Ind Coope (later to become Allied Breweries) as a salesman. He spent twenty-six years with the company, progressing to the post of national sales director. But he never left snooker. 'I had it written into my contract with the brewery that I could continue broadcasting for both the BBC and ITV whenever snooker came on the box,' he says.

Snooker received little or no coverage for seven years. 'The annual broadcasting in 1962 amounted to four fifteen-minute programmes. That year is outstanding because, on one of those four programmes, Joe Davis made the first century on television.'

The seeds for snooker's rapid growth were sown, then scattered, in 1969. 'Right from the Leicester Square Hall days I had pestered the different producers I had become friendly with to put snooker on as a continuity, a series,' explains Ted. 'I told them that if they did, they would have a winner when colour television eventually came along. Nobody would listen to me until one day in 1969 when I got a phone call from Birmingham. A man called Phil Lewis, who was a producer with the BBC, asked if I would put together a series of eight half-hour programmes. I couldn't believe my ears.

'I told him that only one-frame matches would be possible and that the players wouldn't like it. He said: "Well, that's it. Work something out for me. And don't bother about a title, I've got it – it's going to be called *Pot Black*." I said: "Don't be bloody silly. You cannot put a series on television without the word snooker in it; nobody knows the game." But he insisted the name would be *Pot Black* and I was so scared he might cancel, I replied: "Okay, no problem."'

While the idea came from Lewis, it was Ted who developed it and worked out a format. 'There were only eight players in those days, which worked out nicely. I went back to him inside half an hour and said: "Here's your format." Within a matter of a day we had it all sewn up and *Pot Black* went on the air in July 1969.

'Now imagine a snooker programme on television in July. Who is going to watch it? My first thought was that this was going to die a death. In fact, it became a terrific success. So much so that Phil Lewis came back to me and asked me to get it all together again for the November.'

By 1970, *Pot Black* ran for sixteen weeks, and in the following years it was repeated to make thirty-two programmes. Naturally Ted commentated on the matches and was the only person to appear on every show. On the air for eighteen years, the programme was eventually taken off in 1986, a victim of its own success.

Ted admits: 'I never imagined it would be so successful. It was sold all over the world. Even when it was taken off the air it was still drawing an audience of between 10 and 12 million. It was the start of the snooker boom.'

Ted has no doubt about the greatest snooker player he has ever seen, a question he is often asked. 'Without doubt at all, Joe Davis is the greatest snooker player that has ever lived. If you want proof, to start with he was undefeated from 1927 to 1946 in the World Championship.

'The crystalate balls they used at that time were very much heavier than the balls used today. Steve Davis couldn't do half what he does now with the old balls that Joe had to play with. And the pockets have been eased with the undercutting.'

Ted would have trouble placing in order of merit the other players who have reached the top since those days – Fred Davis, Steve Davis, Ray Reardon among others – and is certainly not belittling the achievements of the modern-day Davis. He says: 'I

Man in the middle: Ted Lowe (centre) with (left to right) snooker stars Sidney Smith, Joe Davis, John Pulman and Fred Davis at Ted's birthday party in 1951.

take nothing away from Steve. He has been a great snooker champion, a very worthy champion. But you must also bear in mind that Joe Davis was world billiards champion too.'

Not surprisingly, there have been many highlights during half a century of snooker watching. Dennis Taylor beating Steve Davis on the black to win the 1985 Embassy World Championship is one Ted selects; witnessing Joe Davis make the first maximum 147 break in public in 1955 is another.

While Ted is never happier than pottering around in the garden of his home at Bexhill on the Sussex coast, snooker has taken him all over the world. Like motor-racing's Murray Walker, he has become

famous for his 'Colemanballs' (*Private Eye* magazine's term for commentators' unconsciously 'idiotic' turns of phrase). It was during a pro-celebrity programme on television that he came out with perhaps his best-remembered line.

'It entered my head that there must be millions of people out there who still had black and white sets. As that thought flashed through my mind, I got a full picture on the screen of a snooker that had just been laid. On the spur of the moment I said: "And for those of you watching in black and white, the blue ball is behind the yellow." I didn't realise I had said it until I read it in a newspaper a week later. Of course, it has travelled the world since then!'

HOW THE BENSON AND HEDGES IRISH MASTERS WAS BORN

by Kevin Hughes

Everybody knows that John Spencer won the first ever Irish version of the Benson and Hedges tournament. But how many can accurately recall which player he defeated in the final?

Reference to the snooker record books would inevitably prompt a swift and probably very confident answer that it was Doug Mountjoy, but I'm afraid that's not correct. The carefully chronicled statistics do, indeed, indicate that Spencer beat the recently rejuvenated Welshman in the first final of the Benson and Hedges Irish Masters at Goffs in 1978 to lift the first prize of £1,000. So, why, you will ask, would Mountjoy be an incorrect answer?

It's because that was really something of a trick question in the opening paragraph: I didn't specify that I was referring to the first *Masters* final!

You see, the first Masters tournament at Goffs in 1978 was immediately preceded by a couple of Benson and Hedges Professional Snooker competitions at different venues in the fair city of Dublin. The first – at least, the earliest unearthed through my very extensive investigations – was a one-day spectacular on Saturday, 21 February 1976, staged by the Republic of Ireland Billiards and Snooker Control Council at the National Stadium. It featured former world champions Spencer and

View from the top: A great picture of the snooker arena at Goffs, the horse sales ring that is used as the venue for the Benson and Hedges Irish Masters.

Alex Higgins, along with Dennis Taylor and Graham Miles, and Spencer pocketed the first prize of £600 by whitewashing Higgins in the best-of-nine-frames decider.

What was to become the 'Masters' was therefore established as an annual event when, the following year, again in February, Higgins, Taylor and Miles returned with reigning world champion Ray Reardon. It was now a two-day tournament with a £750 cheque at Leopardstown Race Club. Higgins was the winner on this occasion, defeating Reardon 4–3 in the final.

Actual details of these competitions are sketchy and even the recorded data relating to the first couple of Masters tournaments provide an incomplete picture of the action.

The decision to set up a tournament was taken after the organisers had dipped their toes in to test the water via an exhibition challenge match in 1975. In this Spencer beat Higgins 9–7 in the National Stadium. One of the driving forces behind the Republic's Control Council in those days – and still, even in his eighties, working actively for the benefit of the game in Ireland – was Patrick G. Comerford. A Grade A Referee since 1954, Paddy was proud to officiate at these tournaments.

'As President of the Control Council I helped do the spadework in the beginning and we were heavily involved in the organisation on behalf of Benson and Hedges, unlike today when it's a much bigger promotion handled by professional public relations people,' he recalled. 'Indeed, I well remember that first match in the National Stadium for one particular incident. Radio Telefis Eireann were covering it but they didn't get any pictures of the highest break of the competition because the cameras weren't ready when John Spencer compiled his 120.

'The Stadium wasn't a bad venue. It was capable of holding 2,000 and everyone had a pretty good view because it was purpose-built for boxing and the snooker table was placed in the space where the boxing ring normally was. But in its second year as a tournament we decided to bring it out to Leopardstown to the Race Club, adjacent to where the race meetings are held. It was reasonably successful here, too, but there's no doubt that it really came of age when it was moved yet again in 1978.

'Some people, I recall, feared it might be a mistake that the venue was going out of Dublin into the countryside. But in hindsight it was an inspirational choice, as I'm sure everyone will now agree. This move was to Goffs – and that's where it has been since. In the early years I refereed there with Bill Trulock and Paddy Williams, but later they started to bring over professional referees, starting with

Signed and delivered: The signing ceremony which guaranteed the Benson and Hedges Irish Masters until 1995. Bert Koorn (bottom left), the managing director of Gallaher (Dublin) Ltd, and John Spencer (bottom right), chairman of the WPBSA, study the final details of the £1 million contract. Del Simmons (top left), the WPBSA's marketing executive, and Bill Hartley, the financial director of Goffs, look on.

Irishmen Len Ganley and John Smyth,' remembered Paddy, who still makes a point of attending Goffs and even makes the odd trip to tournaments in Britain.

The man whose brainwave it was to take the event to its present site was Kevin Norton, latterly special events co-ordinator with Benson and Hedges Ireland, but then employed in a very junior position. He doesn't agree that the Leopardstown promotion went off very well.

'To be brutally frank,' he said, 'the saga of Leopardstown will live long in the memory as a wholesale disaster and there was no way the competition was ever going to be staged there again. For starters, the audience was too close to the play and I can still see Ray Reardon complaining bitterly during the final against Higgins about the distracting behaviour of a section of the crowd that just happened to contain a young blonde lady called Lynn, later to become Mrs Alex Higgins.

'So we were on the lookout for somewhere else that could become a permanent home for it. I live in Naas and was even on the site when Goffs was built so I knew the place well. I took the trouble to survey the complex carefully again and was convinced it would make a suitable venue. I recommended to my superiors that they should consider it and the rest is history.'

One of those superiors was Paddy Morgan, who is nowadays landlord of the Railway Bar in Sligo. In the mid-1970s, however, Paddy was the influential promotions manager with Benson and Hedges in Ireland.

'The competition had a very low budget but was becoming very popular,' he recalled. 'The sales ring at Goffs had been used for a couple of variety shows and I had a hunch that the natural amphitheatre would suit the snooker. And it was an instant success.'

A bloodstock sales ring might seem a ridiculous place to stage a major snooker tournament involving all the top players in the world. But it's amazing what an incredible stroke of genius the idea really was. Luxuriously seating 744 people and with adequate standing room for many hundreds more, it is now generally regarded as one of the best arenas on the worldwide snooker circuit. And, despite its pleasant but inconvenient rural setting about 25 miles south of Dublin on what is the main route to the country's second city of Cork, it continually draws large crowds of snooker-starved Irish fans to watch some of the best action of the season.

The initial tournaments at the venue near the quaintly named hamlet of Kill, County Kildare, when the word 'Masters' officially became part of the title, were played on a round-robin basis with six top pros competing for what was still modest prize money: £1,000 to the winner as against the £3,000 Alex Higgins had collected for defeating Cliff Thorburn 7–5 a month earlier in the final of London's ten-man Benson and Hedges Masters equivalent.

'It doesn't sound like an awful lot of money, but it was big in those days. Certainly the players thought so, anyway, and the public were happy to come out in their hundreds to watch them play for it,' insists Kevin, who remembers Graham Miles causing Ireland's top bookmaker of the era, Terry Rogers, a few heart-stopping moments when he made a bold bid for a lucrative maximum break prize. 'Benson and Hedges were offering £1,000 for a 147 and were careful enough to insure themselves against the pay-out by striking a bet of £8 at odds of 125–1 against the break being made. I can still recall the feeling of heart flutters as Graham went for it, but the best he could manage was 135.

'There were some other little incidents that stick in the memory. One of them was in 1986 when Kirk Stevens failed to catch his flight from London for his evening match against Patsy Fagan. I got first word of it at 6.15pm and was trying to organise

Sipping along: Steve Davis who has won the Irish Masters five times.

an exhibition match to substitute. I had made no announcement when, fifteen minutes later, Patsy knocked on my office door. He asked me if it was OK for him to take some of his relatives into the players' lounge. I granted him permission and went to show him where it was only to be confronted by no fewer than sixteen people, all of them very close relatives! He was very grateful and told me he was very hopeful of winning the match. I winked my eye and told him I had no doubt whatsoever that he'd go through to the

---

WHO SAID THAT?

'Some of the things Higgins said to me at the World Cup were unprintable, but there was something said about my late mother Annie which will make me determined to beat him.'

▲

– *Dennis Taylor talking before his quarter-final meeting with Alex Higgins at the Benson and Hedges Irish Masters.*

---

quarter-finals to play Tony Knowles!' laughed Kevin.

Asked who came up with the original proposal to bring the big-name pros over to Dublin, Kevin admitted that he was uncertain, but many other people apparently played a leading role.

'Maurice Hayes was the top dog in management of stars across the water and everything in the sport seemed to revolve around him. The late Dessie Campbell, for example, felt he was the only man who could promote professional snooker in this country and he organised our early shows along with Paddy Thornton, who's also now deceased, and Finbar Ruane and several others who were very active in the local amateur game,' he said.

When the splendid auditorium at Kill was used for the first of the twelve years it's been there, six players were invited and, with three days' play designated, the organisers chose to lengthen the duration by having two sections of three in round-robin competition with the top two players in each group qualifying for knock-out semi-finals.

In that 1978 series the two giants of the time, Ray Reardon and John Spencer, qualified from one section by leaving behind Graham Miles in their wake. Alex Higgins and Doug Mountjoy finished equal in the other half and Higgins toppled the Welshman in a sudden-death shoot-out through a magnificent break of 108. A rare tactical blunder by Higgins, when he was trying to gain prime position on the final black he believed he required, caused him to miss a decisive pink that would have forced a last frame against Spencer and it was the reigning world champion who progressed to the final. Mountjoy stormed back from 0–2 down to snatch victory against fellow-countryman Reardon in the other semi-final, but it was to be Spencer's year for he won the last two frames in emphatic fashion to take the £1,000 cheque.

The following year the round-robin system was used for the last time. Again there were six players but this time a delighted Mountjoy gained ample compensation by winning a thrilling final. He collected £2,000 by coming from 0–3 and 3–5 behind to edge out Reardon, who had missed a simple brown, for a match-winning 6–5 scoreline.

The top prize of £2,500 went to Wales again in 1980, Terry Griffiths completing the Wembley-Goffs double by holding off a late surge by Mountjoy to triumph 9–8. A month earlier in the UK version of the Masters he had clinched a 9–5 win with a 131 clearance against Higgins. And Griffiths was back in both finals in 1981. He set a new tournament record break of 136 at the Conference Centre before losing 6–9 to Higgins, but retained the Irish title and £5,000 through a 9–7 victory over Reardon. Indeed, the pattern was very similar to that twelve months later. After going down 5–9 in the Wembley climax to world champion Steve Davis, Griffiths reversed that result and scoreline in County Kildare, a victory valued in punts for the first time. His sterling return was approximately £6,666. However, the hat-trick was denied the Welshman when he nosedived at the semi-final hurdle as Davis broke his Goffs duck in 1983 with a runaway 9–2 win over Reardon, who suffered his third collapse in the Irish Masters final.

There was an early finish in the following year as well, Davis surviving tough matches against Tony Meo (5–4) and Alex Higgins (6–4) before trouncing Griffiths 9–1 in the decider. Yet there was no hat-trick for the Londoner either. Higgins made sure of that with a 6–2 semi-final success against his arch-rival of the era, but Jimmy White won the 1985 final 9–5.

Patsy Fagan created a major shock the year after that by beating Tony Knowles 5–4 in the quarter-finals, but was whitewashed by defending champion

Jimmy White who proceeded to claim the title a second time by beating Willie Thorne 9–5.

Again three wins in a row seemed a possibility, yet once more it was not to be, for White couldn't get past Thorne in a quarter-final clash in 1987. The Leicester player went on to the final, only to slump to an embarrassing 9–1 setback against a lethal Davis.

It was Benson and Hedges Irish Masters title number 4 for Davis a year later when he swamped Neal Foulds, a cloud hanging over the event after the anticipated invitation to Silvino Francisco did not materialise because of anti-apartheid problems.

The hoodoo that had haunted the home stars in Ireland's only major open professional tournament since it started in Goffs was finally conquered in 1989 – and what a popular winner Higgins proved to be. His first big win since the UK Championship in 1983 had many punters in the packed house in raptures, many others in tears. Still limping after falling from a window, he ditched Cliff Thorburn, Neal Foulds and John Parrott before a revival from 0–4 down enabled him to plot a last-frame final victory over Goffs debutant Stephen Hendry.

As Higgins departed from County Kildare amidst some of the most euphoric scenes ever witnessed there, little did anyone imagine the controversy that would surround his return twelve months later to defend the title! Four days before the Irish Masters came an incredible confrontation between Higgins and team-mate Dennis

Taylor at the British Car Rental World Cup final in Bournemouth. Higgins becoming so enraged during the exchanges that he threatened to have Taylor 'shot' next time he was in Northern Ireland.

And just for good measure, Higgins, as defending champion, was drawn to play the winner of the first-round match between Taylor and Cliff Thorburn in the quarter-final in the 1990 event. That became reality when Taylor easily beat Thorburn and the 'Grudge Match of All Time' was set up on a Friday night that produced one of the most 'memorable occasions' in Irish Masters history.

Tickets were impossible to obtain, even at inflated prices, and media interest increased ten-fold with ITN even sending a top team from London. Taylor insisted that he wanted to win the match for his late mother whose memory he claimed was insulted during Higgins' volley of verbal abuse. The vociferous reception of each player suggested the loyalty of the crowd was equally divided – perhaps a triumph for Taylor as Higgins had always been the clearly acknowledged favourite here.

The match was tense throughout, and several times the attitude of the spectators threatened to cause tempers to fray, with Higgins, at one stage, making a fervent appeal for their best behaviour. This was viewed by some observers as more of an attempt to restrain his own emotions. The crowd's tremendous relief and delight when their particular hero clinched a frame was almost palpable, and sometimes visual evidence of this was demonstrated by the respective protagonists too. But in the end there was no verbal or physical contact, apart from the customary handshakes at the beginning and end of a match that Taylor comfortably won 5–2.

The Blackburn-based Irishman went on to conquer Jimmy White to reach his first final in this tournament, but he proved no match for Steve Davis, a convincing 9–4 victor – and Irish Masters champion for the fifth time.

This season's competition will have to be special to surpass the excitement, drama and thrills of 1990, but whatever happens it's sure to be one of the memorable weeks in the snooker calendar. It always is.

The moment of truth: Alex Higgins (left) and Dennis Taylor shake hands before their quarter-final match in the 1990 Benson and Hedges Irish Masters.

How Dripping Water Helped the Career of Referee John Williams

John Williams, one the game's most respected referees, certainly remembers the lucky break that changed his career in 1973.

He recalls: 'I was just one of more than forty referees officiating at the World Championship at the City Exhibition Hall in Manchester. I was virtually unknown and I think they must have got my name muddled up with a Grade A referee when I was asked to take charge of the quarter-final match between Alex Higgins and Fred Davis.

'Then in the middle of the match rain started dripping down on to the table as Fred was about to clear up the last three colours to win a frame. There was no way we could carry on and it was Alex who suggested that we mark where the balls were with a piece of chalk and leave the arena. It was certainly a case of rain stopped play.

'The problem turned out to be a crack in the glass roof which had happened while they were blacking it out so that daylight could not get in. In the end they patched it up and we got on with the game. But everybody remembered that incident and the next year I was invited back to officiate at Belle Vue in Manchester and I have been lucky enough to be present at every World Championship since.'

John was born on 8 June 1937 in Ruabon in North Wales – a village that also produced Mark Hughes, the Manchester United and Welsh International striker. One of six children (three sisters and three brothers), John attended the local Church of England school where he was bright enough to pass his eleven plus when only nine years old. Cricket, soccer and, inevitably, because of his Welsh heritage, rugby were John's sporting loves. He played right-half at soccer and also had an amateur trial for Wales.

His dad, Ted, worked as a fanhouse attendant at Gresford Colliery but there was no mining life for John. When he left school at seventeen with seven 'O' levels, he went to work as a trainee metallurgist to carry out tests in the steel industry. He was asked to travel to play for the once-famous Bolton Wanderers as an amateur but he could never get there because he could manage only one Saturday off in every four weeks from his job.

In charge: John Williams.

John also played snooker in the local village club, which housed three tables, and eventually made a career best break of 73 which was good enough to establish him in League snooker in North Wales. By this time he had married Joyce and they had four children – Stephen (now thirty-one), Barry (twenty-nine), Neil (twenty-seven) and Janet (seventeen).

John's refereeing career began in the early 1970s when they had a qualifying round of the Welsh Amateur Championship at the Llay Royal British Legion Club in Wrexham. There was no marker and John stepped in to look after the scores. Later he bought a rule book and set about becoming a referee.

It was then that he struck up a

Famous five: (left to right) John Street, Vic Bartlam, Len Ganley, Alan Chamberlain and John Williams look immaculate despite the 100°F-plus heat outside the Al Nasr Stadium in Dubai.

friendship with John Powell, who later became chairman of the Welsh Sports Council, but at the time was president of the Welsh Billiards and Snooker Association. Williams was also instrumental in setting up the North Wales Billiards and Snooker Association in 1974 and soon snooker, unbeknown to him, was to take over his life. He had changed jobs by now and was working on quality control at Pilkington Glass, but that job didn't last long and it was then that he joined the Civil Service as an executive officer in the Department of Employment in Wrexham.

After his lucky break in the 1973 World Championship, John was one of four referees asked by Ted Lowe, BBC's top commentator, to officiate at the first Pontin's Festival – an event which is now one of the longest-running tournaments on the circuit.

John remembers: 'It was absolutely chaotic and I just didn't know how we managed to get all the games played. But it must have gone OK because I have been every year since, although it has got a lot easier over the years.

'Pontin's has been the starting ground for so many players, like Steve Davis, Terry Griffiths, Jimmy White, Willie Thorne and John Parrott. In fact, virtually everybody in the game has played at Prestatyn in North Wales at some time or another.'

John was by this time spending a lot of time on snooker refereeing and that's when the crunch came. He says: 'I had to decide whether to become a snooker referee full-time because staff cuts were being made in the Civil Service and that could have meant I could not get so much time off. I opted for snooker and gave up my job in 1981. Luckily, it worked out for me and I have had steady employment in snooker ever since.'

A 147 maximum is obviously a landmark for any professional player and the same can be said for a referee. John was

Keeping watch: Referee John Williams and Mike Hallett at the 555 Asian Open in Bangkok.

Out of this world: Russian cosmonaut Victor Liakhov popped in for a flying visit at the Dubai Duty Free Classic. The referees are (left to right) John Williams, Alan Chamberlain, Vic Bartlam and John Street.

Heads or tails?: John Williams waits for the call before the match with Steve Davis (left) and Willie Thorne in the Benson and Hedges Irish Masters.

fortunate enough to be the man in charge when Cliff Thorburn scored a 147 during the World Championship at the Crucible Theatre in 1983.

He recalls: 'It was a wonderful occasion and it's still in the record books as the only maximum at the World Championship. It is now part of snooker history and I can look back and say "I was there" every time it's shown on television.'

That 147 was certainly a moment to remember, but what has been his greatest moment in snooker? 'There is no doubt about that,' he says. 'It has to be the Dennis Taylor and Steve Davis world final in 1985 which Dennis won 18–17 on the final black. It was a match that anybody who loves snooker will never forget and I was just proud to be part of such a memorable occasion.'

Williams, thanks to snooker's overseas 'explosion', has travelled extensively, especially during the past couple of years when he has visited Hong Kong, Thailand, Dubai, France and Canada. He says: 'I used to get over to Europe to places like Belgium or Spain for the odd weekend but now we spend a lot of time overseas. I love the travelling, I love the people and I love being with the snooker players and officials, but I must be honest – I don't get on with the local food. I would rather have bacon and eggs or steak and chips any time and for me eating abroad can sometimes be a bit of a problem.'

Of course, referees sometimes make mistakes and John, after all, is only human. His worst moment, he recalls, 'was in the 1980 Coral UK Championship final between Davis and Higgins. Davis had just potted a pink and I was working out whether it would go back on its spot when for some reason I just picked up the white ball. Davis was killing himself laughing and I just wished a hole in the ground could have swallowed me up as I stood there with the cue ball in my hand. Amazingly Alex tried to claim a foul. That's probably the worst moment I have ever gone through, but it's something now that I can look back on and laugh about.'

John is now divorced and remarried – to Kathleen with whom he lives in a semi-detached house in Shrewsbury. Snooker refereeing is a very demanding life so how does John relax? He jokes: 'I indulge in "automatic" gardening. I can transform the wilderness of my garden into a lovely flowering area in about half a day. I just go down to the garden centre, buy loads of flowering plants and stick them in the ground!'

CAN YOU WIN AGAINST WIZARD WILLIAMS?

John Williams has travelled the world as a snooker referee. Here he sets a fun quiz to check out your knowledge of snooker and billiards. Some questions are easy, some are hard, and there's one that John is sure will catch you out. Write down your answers and then turn to page 140 to find out if you will ever be good enough to become a professional referee.

1 When is the only time during a live frame of snooker that a player may pick up the cue ball from the bed of the table without being penalised?

2 What is the minimum length of a cue?

3 At the beginning of a frame of snooker the blue ball is left in a pocket. A player is on a break and has made 26 when the error is spotted. What happens next?

4 Player A is disqualified for unfair conduct and the frame score at the time is: player A, 18 points; player B, 11 points. There are nine reds remaining. What frame score goes into the record books?

5 A player pots a red and the cue ball then jumps over the remaining reds. What is the decision?

6 The red is ball-on and the cue ball is touching the red. The player plays away from the red but it has been balancing on a chalk mark on the cloth. This results in the red ball moving even though the player is playing away from it. What is the referee's verdict?

7 Here is a billiards question. Player A is on a break and his white ball comes to rest touching his opponent's white. What happens next?

8 A player is undecided whether the cue ball will go through a gap between two other balls. He takes a red out of a pocket to check whether it will pass. What is the decision?

9 When is a player entitled to ask the referee for physical assistance in the playing of a shot?

10 A player plays a shot on a red and the cue ball leaves the bed of the table and comes to rest on the cushion rail. What does the referee do?

A Thai in Bradford: James Wattana
by Bob Holmes

James Wattana does not have to read Rudyard Kipling to know that East is East and West is West. Anyone who divides his year between Downtown Bangkok and the outskirts of Bradford is unlikely to have illusions about that. Only when the cultural chasm between these two 'ends of the earth' is fully appreciated does the twenty-year-old Thai's achievement in reaching the top flight in his first season as a professional snooker player begin to sink in.

Indeed, it is doubtful if Kipling — even at his most lyrical — could have found two more diverse locations than the teeming dockland of Thailand's capital, where

Local hero: James Wattana before a match in the 555 Asian Open in his home city of Bangkok.

Wattana's home is, and the bleak wilderness of Ilkley Moor, which his current base overlooks. Yet, ironically, it is here, in the flat behind a pub which his manager and mentor Tom Moran bought ten years ago as a *pied-à-terre* for watching Yorkshire cricket, that Wattana is beginning to come to terms with Western ways. And judging by his performances on the table, his burgeoning vocabulary and increasing ability to cope single-handedly with press conferences, it is proving an inspired if unlikely choice.

However, even with the wise counselling of fellow pros Joe Johnson and Marcel Gauvreau, who are, like him, based at the nearby Cuedos Club; with a glimpse of the Brontë country from his bedroom window and a BMW in which to spin over its rugged contours, Wattana is a most reluctant 'Yorkshireman'.

'Sometimes I miss home so bad,' he says, 'that I wish I was not a snooker player. Bradford is so quiet that living here is like being at a funeral — I often get bored, but I just accept it. It is not my home and it's as simple as that.' Does he like Britain? 'Not really,' he admits, chuckling at his own naivety. 'I thought it was going to be like what I'd seen on TV and in the movies — it's a big disappointment.'

But if Wattana's views are unusually forthright for an Oriental, he is not ungracious when it comes to acknowledging all the help he has had in these parts — or the friendliness of local folk. 'I like the people very much — they have been very kind to me,' he says. 'A fortune teller once told me that somebody would always look after me and up to now someone always has.'

Manager Moran has assumed that role in

earnest, but there are others without whom the intrepid cuemaster's attempts to negotiate the treacherous path to professionalism would surely have foundered. And if Wattana's lack of appreciation for things British – he does not drink and lists cricket, scenery, most English and Indian foods, reading and the low tempo of our lives among his pet hates – is not entirely surprising for one reared in more tumultuous confines, you only have to think of how Western snooker rookies might have fared had they been forced to make their way in Thailand.

Proud parents: James Wattana with mum and dad.

And those sceptics who have been swift to point out that the Thai's failure to reach the World Championship proper indicates that he is hardly the stuff of a Wonder Boy are overlooking what, in the eyes of more rational judges, have to be regarded as mitigating circumstances. Indeed, the fact that his finest hour last season was in front

Early days: A younger Wattana with his mother and sister at the family temple in Thailand.

of his adoring compatriots – when he reached the final of the 555 Asian Open in Bangkok – is further evidence that in cooler climes a tropical flower requires more tender nurturing.

Shortcomings in Wattana's game, however, are another matter, and while whispers about his shot selection and safety play have become increasingly audible, they are countered by comments from those who ought to know. 'He plays shots that took me five years to work out,' admits regular practice partner Gauvreau, and none other than Steve Davis declares: 'Looking around at all the players and not just the youngsters, I would say that Wattana is one with the potential to go right to the top.'

If additional affidavits are required, one need look no further than the way in which Wattana obtained his pro ticket in the first place. 'I think that was my greatest achievement,' he declares, still apparently bewildered by his conquest of the amateur game in 1988/89 when he won the Asian and World Championships *and* earned his pro ticket. But he adds: 'I just don't know how I did it.' Head still shaking, he winces at the memory of cold showers in holiday camps, spartan, phoneless chalets and the food – oh, the food! – not to mention the humbling experience of having to do his own marking after being accustomed to the five-star luxuries of the Asian circuit.

'I've been playing for money since I was ten,' he admits. 'Thais love to gamble and older people would come into my mother's club and take me on. I only took up the game at nine, but I could beat most of them. The problem was they sometimes did not pay me – snooker is still a game for bad people in Thailand.' If he did not have the muscle to extract his winnings at that tender age, Wattana acquired the rudiments of the game in a tougher school than his Western contemporaries cosseted by snooker's new-found respectability.

Star line-up: James Wattana (right) and the world's top three (left to right), Stephen Hendry, Steve Davis and John Parrott.

He had displayed a rare streak of defiance to pick up a cue. 'Even though my mother owned a club,' he laughs, 'she did not want me to be a snooker player. She hoped I would go to university instead!' When his chuckles subsided, he recalled: 'There used to be fights in the club, usually over table fees; sometimes people would cut the cloth. But my mother was a tough lady and she handled all the trouble – she had divorced my father by then.'

So Tong, as Wattana is known in Thailand, enjoyed the classic 'Jimmy White' apprenticeship of taking time off school and money off mugs – all of which was to stand him in good stead when the full 'price' of mis-spending his late teens had to be met. And, like White, he enjoyed some memorable moments.

The most lucrative spell Wattana had was around the age of fifteen when a pal staked the rough equivalent of £100 on him to beat all comers. 'We went on a tour and my friend did all the talking, but he did not pretend I was a bad player,' he insists. 'It was not really hustling, but I just took on everybody and beat them until I ran out of opponents. We won about £12,000 in three weeks. I gave half to my mother for an air-conditioner for her club and spent the rest on jewellery, on clothes, on drink, on – you name it. We had a good time.'

Having enjoyed a taste of wealth in a country where the average per capita income is £500 per year, Wattana could no longer discover anyone good enough to give him a game, but a year later, in the Camus Masters, he found himself up against Terry Griffiths, Dennis Taylor and Steve Davis, all of whom he disdainfully dismissed on the way to the title. As the Thais began to celebrate the arrival of their potting wizard, Wattana, to his credit, was not kidded: 'None of them were near their best,' he admitted, 'when they played me.'

No matter: his performances were still sufficiently persuasive for leading local officials to seek to further his education, and the now-deceased Maurice Kerr, then president of the Thai Snooker Association, prevailed upon a Chester resident called Harry Wah to offer the young man accommodation to enable him to learn English and polish his game. Kerr's kindness notwithstanding, it was a harsh baptism, and though Wattana enjoyed playing Nick Dyson in the local club, the return half of his ticket was never going to be wasted.

He went back ostensibly for the Asian Open but, glad to be reacquainted with

Question time: James Wattana (right) and manager Tom Moran answer questions during the 555 Asian Open.

warmer climes, stayed six months before a renewed order to 'Go West, young man' saw him ensconced in the Sussex home of a wealthy Hong Kong Chinese who had connections with his family. Once again the confines – in the poshest part of Brighton – were comfortable, even luxurious, but no substitute for home.

'Life was too good,' says Wattana. 'We

had plenty of money and we would go to casinos and blow it. We met a lot of Chinese people and drank quite a bit too. It was good, but no good. In the end I was owed some cash and left to join my brother who was in a bedsit in London. I had no money, nothing to eat and we shared a tiny room — an area about half the size of my current lounge in Bradford. It was cold, crowded — barely the size of a snooker table, with a wardrobe and sink — and conditions were very bad. It was the worst time in my life and I couldn't wait to get home. I swore I'd never come back. Never.'

Wild horses appeared in the shape of Moran, a Bradford-born engineer who had lived in Thailand for over twenty years, become a Thai citizen and really was the only man who could have swayed the disillusioned youngster into giving the centre of the snooker kingdom one last try. But Moran did not pressurize Wattana — his mother did. 'She was determined that I should go again,' he insists, now clearly amused by his mother's change of heart. 'I did not want to go and told my brothers and sister. You cannot argue with your parents in Thailand until you're twenty-one.'

However, the Thai Snooker Association had convinced his mother that her son was, indeed, a wonder boy, and agreed to pay his fare. When Moran, whose mastery of Thai, urbane manner and quietly reassuring man-management skills had already persuaded Wattana to sign a contract,

offered his empty pad just a couple of miles from the practice facilities at Cuedos, the lad agreed to have another go, albeit reluctantly.

Study in concentration: James Wattana.

Now Wattana is regularly mobbed on arrival home, was Thailand's Sportsman of the Year and has had the main news bulletin of the evening postponed by prime ministerial decree — just to let the nation watch him complete a frame!

Moran is concerned that Wattana, who spends most of his time watching videos on a 44-inch screen, is not only estranged from his family — his sister Tuk and brother Tik manage Mum's club while Tam, his other brother, runs another club — but also from his girlfriend Aay and is leading a somewhat unnatural existence. 'There is not enough gaiety in his life — he does not laugh very much,' says the manager who is well aware that Wattana's base, which is fine for a middle-aged, cricket-loving Yorkshireman, is not ideal for a twenty-year-old snooker-playing Thai. 'But perhaps that's the way it's got to be,' he adds. 'Hard.'

Wattana, whose £50,000 sponsorship from Nestlé and first year's winnings of £64,000 help soften the grind, accepts that. Already well on the way to buying a dream house in Bangkok for his family, he knows that the view from his window is far from bleak. Even on the darkest days he can see a vision of the East.

ALLISON FISHER: A TALENTED YOUNG WOMAN IN A MAN'S WORLD

by Alexander Clyde

She is small and blonde with clear blue eyes, a snub nose and an infectious giggle. But appearances can sometimes be deceptive, because there is nothing of the little girl lost about Ms Allison Fisher. Emmeline Pankhurst and her friends would be both pleased and proud, if they were alive today, to see how their modern counterpart in the suffragette movement is fighting to haul down the men-only barriers in the ever-so-male world of professional snooker. Without resorting to chaining herself to any railings outside a snooker club or flinging herself in front of a Jimmy White long pot at the Crucible, Allison Fisher persuaded the snooker hierarchy into putting her name forward for membership of their association.

Sadly the rank and file membership failed to support the proposal at an extraordinary general meeting of the World Professional Billiards and Snooker Association during last season's Embassy World Championship at Sheffield. Having had her hopes raised and then dashed that she would become the first female to be allowed to compete alongside the men on the professional snooker circuit, the four-times women's world champion and undoubted Queen of the Green Baize had to swallow her disappointment. The members had, in fact, voted 69–39 in favour of

Star duo: Allison Fisher and Stephen Hendry show off their trophies after beating American pair Steve Mizerak and Ewa Mataya in the Continental Airlines Snooker/Pool Challenge.

Ms Fisher's acceptance, but that figure fell short of the 75 per cent majority needed.

She even talked about quitting if she did not obtain her pro ticket by the end of next season. However, Ms Fisher's career suddenly took off in a most unexpected way as she was signed on a five-year management contract by Barry Hearn's Matchroom organisation, and then in July 1990 the game's professionals voted for the game to go 'open' which means that Allison will be on the circuit for the 1991/92 season. 'I will make Allison the first millionairess in snooker within five years,' was Hearn's proud boast, while Allison, after signing the contract at London's Cafe Royal, commented: 'This is the greatest day of my career.' A range of cues, tables and accessories were being planned for her. Ironically Allison had written to Hearn

The big day: Allison Fisher celebrates with champagne after signing a five-year contract with Barry Hearn's Matchroom organisation.

when she was fourteen asking him for sponsorship. He had turned her down, and now remarked: 'If someone had said to me five years ago that I'd be signing a female player, I'd have said they were crazy.'

Allison will have her future career mapped out for her by Hearn, though to get this far she has faced obstacles every step of the way on her long and winding road towards her great ambition – to become a member of the WPBSA and lead the emancipation of snooker into the twenty-first century. She is a mighty determined young lady, a quality which shines through her snooker as well as in her attitude to her chosen profession. The fact that she is a female – a bright and attractive one, at that – will win her huge commercial benefits. According to Hearn: 'After Stephen Hendry, Steve Davis and Jimmy White, Allison is probably the most marketable property in snooker.'

She collected her first world title when she was only seventeen, she is the best female player the game has ever seen and clearly has the potential – with a nice blend of natural ability and fierce determination – to make a decent impact on the professional circuit. The fact is that, up to now, having played the game full-time since leaving school, she earns a decidedly modest income, probably less than men who are ranked in the lower levels on the WPBSA circuit. Her biggest pay cheque was £3,500 for winning the women's world title and her earnings last season were £24,000.

Allison was bitten by the snooker bug at the tender age of seven, was competing against men in her local Sussex league at thirteen and had made up her mind at fifteen that she was going to be the trail blazer, the first woman to compete on equal terms against men in the professional snooker jungle.

Snooker is unlike physical sports such as soccer, rugby and cricket, where men's superior physical strength will always give

Champ again: Allison Fisher collects her trophy and bouquet after beating Ann-Marie Farren in the final of the Pontin's World Ladies Championship. Rich Harper is the Pontin's man in the middle.

them a clear advantage. And Allison has the perfect answer to those chauvinists who shake their heads and mutter that women are . . . well, you know, the wrong shape to wield a snooker cue in the correct fashion across their chests. 'They tell me the women can't play properly because of their shape,' she smiles. 'I tell them that hasn't stopped Bill Werbeniuk.' Dolly Parton and other similarly constructed ladies might struggle to hold a cue correctly but Ms Fisher, Stacey Hillyard and Ann-Marie Farren, the three leading female players, have what can be tactfully described as 'neat' figures.

Allison has a top break of 144 and no less a judge than the legendary Frank Callan, who has coached her since she was sixteen, reckons she has the talent to make

it to the upper echelons of the game. When it comes to measuring the ability of a snooker player, you argue with this wise old owl at your peril!

Allison was born on 24 February 1968 at Cheshunt in Hertfordshire (a birthplace she shares, incidentally, with the Peter Pan of Pop, Cliff Richard). 'I'm a Piscean so, apparently, I'm dreamy and creative,' she laughs. When she was four, the young Queen of Herts moved with her parents Peter and Christine and older brothers David and Simon to Thames Ditton in Surrey. They lived there for seven years before heading for Peacehaven, near Brighton on the Sussex coast, where Allison lived from the age of eleven until she was twenty-one, when she bought her own place at Hadlow, a village in Kent on the A26, between Tonbridge and Sevenoaks.

Stranglehold: John Parrott jokingly tries to 'kill' off Allison Fisher after she beat him in an exhibition match.

Allison recalls: 'I was a bit of a tomboy, probably because I had two big brothers. I first saw snooker on television when I was about seven. I was watching *Pot Black* and it seemed to click with me. I liked the look of it and asked my parents for a table. It was only a miniature one, a 2-foot, but I was intrigued by the game and didn't see why it had to be a game for boys only.'

She progressed to a 6-foot table that her father bought her when she was eleven. As she told Jean Rafferty (author of that splendidly honest book *The Cruel Game*) in the 1987 *Benson and Hedges Snooker Year:* 'I remember when I was eight and a bridesmaid at a wedding. There were five of us and we went downstairs to this full-sized snooker table. They said to me: "You score," But I didn't want to score, I wanted to play. Another time, I was told I couldn't play on the table at the Peacehaven Social Club, where my mum and dad were members. I was crying in my bed that night when my mum came in and asked me: "What's wrong?" I told her: "I wanted to play on that table." So they persuaded the club to let me use it. It was me desperately wanting to do it. It's strange.'

It therefore came as no surprise that, when Allison was eleven, she went along to a children's coaching clinic at Worthing Snooker Centre, run by Frank Sandell and guest coach Jim Meadowcroft, now best known as an ITV commentator. The fact that she was the only girl among a crowd of boys did not daunt little Ms Fisher.

By the time she was thirteen, Allison was playing against men in her local snooker league and it was clear that she was something special. Her parents did

nothing but encourage their daughter to pursue her unusual vocation and, when it became obvious that she had real potential, Mr and Mrs Fisher took out a second mortgage for an extension on their home to accommodate Allison's snooker room, complete with full-sized table.

At fifteen she was competing in the UK Women's Championships and Frank Callan was among the spectators. Allison takes up the story: 'Frank got chatting to my parents and the next thing I knew he was giving me some coaching. He helped me more in two days than all the rest of the time put together. Frank made my cue action more steely, smoother and more deliberate.'

When she was eighteen, she signed up with Fred Cook's Metro Computers company of Welling, in Kent. It was a three-year contract which earned her a salary, expenses, sponsored car and use of the table at the company's headquarters.

Allison became more high-profile. She won the Tie Woman of the Year award and made her first pilgrimage to the Crucible Theatre in Sheffield during the 1988 Embassy World Championship. She watched some matches and sat in the chairs where the players had sat for the final. 'I couldn't believe how small the arena was,' she recalls. 'The atmosphere was terrific and I'm glad I sampled it because I hope to be going back there as a player and I'll know what to expect.'

The disappointment of narrowly missing out in the 1988 pro-ticket play-offs was a big setback and she slipped down the

Top woman: Allison Fisher in action during an exhibition tour of Canada.

amateur rankings. Having been in the top twenty-four, she was struggling for a place in the top hundred a year later, such is the intensity of the competition among the hungry young amateurs clamouring for places on the professional circuit.

She parted with Fred Cook and she was looked after by her father until Barry Hearn arrived on the scene. Peter Fisher acted as a combination of chaperone, driver, business adviser and minder for a year and accompanied her on two gruelling tours of Canada and one to Bermuda ('I was so busy playing and travelling that I hardly had time to go to the beach,' she laughs). He also travelled with her all through last season, when she was contracted to Barry Hearn to play warm-up matches against local club champions in StormSeal Match-room League fixtures at various venues around Britain.

She insists that she has no particular heroes but it is no coincidence that the two players she admires most are Steve Davis and Stephen Hendry. She says: 'Steve Davis is so good in all aspects of his game, he's so professional in every way. He's also very nice, as anyone who actually knows him will tell you.

'Stephen Hendry's certainly got his head screwed on. He knows how important it is to keep contact with your friends, the real friends that you had before getting involved in snooker. They keep your feet on the ground.'

Now snooker has finally gone 'open' Allison will compete alongside men on the professional snooker circuit, but it is a little-known fact that she would not be the first lady to be elected a member of the WPBSA. That honour was accorded to the legendary Joyce Gardner, but hers was more of an honorary position and she never actually competed against the men.

DID YOU WAVER AGAINST THE WIZARDRY OF WILLIAMS?
Answers to the questions on page 129

1 When he is angled after a foul. He is entitled to pick up the cue ball and play from hand. *(Score 7 points.)*

2 Three feet. *(Score 3 points.)*

3 The blue is placed on its spot, or the highest spot available if the centre spot is occupied, and the break continues. *(Score 5 points.)*

4 Player A, 0 points; player B, 110 points. *(Score 5 points.)*

5 Fair stroke. *(Score 4 points.)*

6 Fair stroke. *(Score 6 points.)*

7 The red ball is placed on its spot and his opponent's white is placed on the centre spot. The player plays from hand and his break continues. *(Score 4 points.)*

8 Foul – penalty, 7 points. *(Score 5 points.)*

9 If the light shade is in the way, a player is entitled to ask the referee to move it while he plays his shot. *(Score 8 points.)*

10 The referee declares a foul – penalty, 4 points – and picks up the cue ball for the next player to play from hand. *(Score 3 points.)*

How did you manage?

 0–10: Have you ever thought about taking up underwater knitting?

 11–20: Getting better – just take up ordinary knitting!

 21–30: Things are improving – you can referee down your local club.

 31–40: Now this is more like it – I'll see you in Sheffield.

 41–50: Brilliant – do you want a job?

THE WAY THEY WERE . . . BUT WHO ARE THEY?
Identification of the photographs of budding snooker champions on pages 62–3

1 Dennis Taylor.
2 John Parrott.
3 Steve Davis.
4 Willie Thorne.

5 Mike Hallett.
6 Neal Foulds.
7 Stephen Hendry.

SNOOKER SNIPPETS

THE OLDEST PLAYER ON THE CIRCUIT

Fred Davis, at seventy-seven, is the oldest full-time player on the professional circuit. Fred first joined the professional ranks in 1930. He has won the world snooker title eight times.

THE PLAYER OF THE SEASON

There was only one contender – Stephen Hendry, the world champion, world number 1 and Associate Editor of the Benson and Hedges Snooker Year.

Simply great: Stephen Hendry (left) and Mick Hucknall, lead singer of rock group Simply Red, at the reception following Hendry's World Championship victory.

THE HAIRCUT OF THE SEASON

That just had to be the balding Willie Thorne who, at one stage, decided to wear his remaining hair in a pony-tail!

Striking pair: Willie Thorne (here, right, with locks flowing free!) and his best friend Gary Lineker, England's number 1 striker.

THE LONGEST MATCH OF THE SEASON

Cliff Thorburn and Doug Mountjoy battled it out for twelve hours, thirty-seven minutes in the second round of the Embassy World Championship in Sheffield before Thorburn won 13–12. The twenty-third frame lasted sixty minutes, though Thorburn is no stranger to long matches as he took part in the latest finish at the World Championship: 3.51am, when he played Terry Griffiths in 1983.

THE MOST UNUSUAL BREAK OF THE SEASON

Steve James compiled the first 'sixteen red' clearance in tournament history during his 10–5 Embassy World Championship first-round victory over Alex Higgins. James took a free ball, fifteen reds and all the colours for a total of 135.

THE BIGGEST CROWD OF THE SEASON

The Wembley Conference Centre produced the largest attendance of the season when 2,740 spectators crowded in to see the last session of the Benson and Hedges Masters final in which Stephen Hendry beat John Parrott 9–4.

THE CHANGING FACE OF BILLIARDS

Professional billiards has, for many years, lived in the shadow of snooker but that does not mean there is no interest in the three-ball game. On the contrary, billiards has managed to survive, and proof of the desire to maintain its place as the 'senior' cue sport is the fact that young players, particularly from the Teesside area, continue to develop and take their place in the professional game. Of course, no professional billiards player is going to reap the rich rewards awaiting the top snooker players, but there is money to be made in tournaments like the British Open, the Strachan UK Championship and the World Championship.

There have been tentative steps to create a relationship between English billiards and Carom billiards, the Continental version which does not require the use of pockets but concentrates on cannons, the most difficult of which is the three-cushion cannon. At the time of writing, Strachan, a generous and long-standing supporter of billiards, was planning a Carom Championship in the UK to be staged at the same time as their UK Championship in 1990. It is an ambitious project but one that is needed if the so-called lesser cue sports like billiards are to have a viable future.

Mark Wildman, a former world professional billiards champion, was instrumental in setting up the contact with the Carom representatives. Last season Wildman paid a visit to a Carom World Team Championship in Essen, West Germany, which was combined with the first International Billiard Trade Fair. He said: 'There were three tables in operation – they were playing one-cushion cannons, three-cushion cannons and a complicated game called Cadre 71/2. There were teams from as far afield as Argentina and Japan and there was also a pool championship being played at the same time. The attendances were quite spectacular and, over the final two days, there were 20,000 spectators who paid £165,000 in gate money.' Those figures are remarkable and are far in excess of what snooker would expect to get in the UK.

On the amateur scene the Teesside Boys Billiards League continues to churn out winners. The North East is certainly a hotbed of billiards, though the North West in the Widnes area is also beginning to produce a fine crop of youngsters.

While snooker dominates the television screen and other media, billiards is far from finished. All over the UK, billiards leagues are in operation, young players are still coming into the game and the sport is ticking over nicely – though cash injections from major sponsors would be a very nice bonus. Of course, television coverage would greatly help the projection of billiards and, though BBC and ITV have flirted with screening the occasional tournament, the immediate vacuum could be filled by satellite television.

BRITISH OPEN CHAMPIONSHIP

Mike Russell was expected to sweep everything before him in the 1989/90 season. After all, he was world champion and had won four of the five titles on offer in the previous season. The one title that had eluded him was the British Open. Yet the Open was to pass Russell by again as Peter Gilchrist, in his second year as a professional, regained the title he won so well in Middlesbrough the year before. This time the Excelsior Club in Leeds was the venue for his 1,166–1,008 final victory over Norman Dagley, a former world champion.

Russell, from Marske, near Redcar, had departed in the first round when India's Geet Sethi compiled an excellent 444 break in beating Russell 1,073–557. Sethi, however, did not survive the quarter-final as he went down 650–423 to Gilchrist.

There were upsets like Eugene Hughes' 10-point win over Australia's Rob Foldvari, a former world champion, which Hughes followed by beating seventy-six-year-old Fred Davis 638–473 to reach the semi-final. Hughes, better known for his snooker exploits, is no mug when it comes to the three-ball game, having won the Irish Amateur Championship in 1977 and 1978.

Dagley ended Hughes' hopes 1,505–903 in the last four, while Gilchrist had to scrap to get through against local player Ian Williamson who, at one stage, trailed by nearly 400 points. In the end a relieved Gilchrist came through 935–827.

The final was similar, with Gilchrist building up large leads which the experienced Dagley whittled away. A 252 break helped move Dagley to within 27 points before Gilchrist pulled away to take the £3,000 first prize by a margin of 158 points.

British Open Championship Results

FIRST ROUND:	N. Dagley (Eng) bt H. Nimmo (Scot) 615–368; C. Everton (Wales) w/o M. Ferreira (India); F. Davis (Eng) bt R. Edmonds (Eng) 493–409; E. Hughes (Rep Ire) bt R. Foldvari (Aust) 400–390; I. Williamson (Eng) bt J. Murphy (Eng) 566–305; R. Close (Eng) w/o M. Wildman (Eng); P. Gilchrist (Eng) bt S. Naisby (Eng) 639–510; G. Sethi (India) bt M. Russell (Eng) 1,073–557 Losers: £150
QUARTER-FINALS:	Dagley bt Everton 685–332; Hughes bt Davis 638–473; Williamson bt Close 501–329; Gilchrist bt Sethi 650–423 Losers: £500
SEMI-FINALS:	Dagley bt Hughes 1,505–903; Gilchrist bt Williamson 935–827 Losers: £1,000
FINAL:	Gilchrist bt Dagley 1,166–1,008 Loser: £1,500 Winner: £3,000

High break: 444 – G. Sethi £300

STRACHAN UK CHAMPIONSHIP

Proof that Teesside is the 'capital' of world billiards was provided in the final of the Strachan UK Championship when yet another young star, Johnny Murphy, from Hartlepool, reached the final in his first season on the circuit. Murphy, then twenty-one, beat the veteran Jack Kar- nehm, former world professional champions Norman Dagley and Ray Edmonds and the experienced Bob Close. In the final he met the defending champion, Mike Russell. It turned out to be a fascinating encounter. Murphy was certainly not disgraced and kept biting away at Russell's lead until the title holder pulled away towards the end to win 1,478–1,058.

There was a moment of billiards history in the preliminary round match between Murphy and Karnehm when they finished the match all square at 487–487 after Karnehm ran out of time with an unfinished break of 82. It was the first time anybody could remember when a match had been tied and 'extra time' of 30 minutes was played, with Murphy coming home by 8 points.

Murphy went on to beat Dagley in the second round, and the latter commented: 'Murphy played wonderfully well and his break of 224 was lovely to watch, full of gentle strokes and control' – praise indeed from such a fine competitor as Dagley.

Russell produced some memorable moments in his 1,973–1,014 defeat of Peter Gilchrist in the semi-final. After the first session Russell had scored five centuries and a break of 220 to lead 978–310 and, though Gilchrist inevitably recovered, Russell compiled an excellent 268 –

Magic Mike: Mike Russell with his Strachan UK Championship trophy.

the highest of the tournament – for a comfortable win.

Strachan UK Championship Results

FIRST ROUND:	M. Russell (Eng) bt M. Wildman (Eng) 679–571; E. Charlton (Aust) bt E. Hughes (Rep Ire) 633–235; P. Gilchrist (Eng) bt G. Thompson (Eng) 640–487; C. Everton (Wales) bt R. Foldvari (Aust) 365–337; I. Williamson (Eng) bt F. Davis (Eng) 533–252; R. Edmonds (Eng) bt H. Nimmo (Scot) 673–451; R. Close (Eng) bt D. Edwards (Wales) 680–455; J. Murphy (Eng) bt N. Dagley (Eng) 693–531 Losers: £150
QUARTER-FINALS:	Russell bt Charlton 750–417; Gilchrist bt Everton 863–264; Edmonds bt Williamson 457–390; Murphy bt Close 492–455 Losers: £500
SEMI-FINALS:	Russell bt Gilchrist 1,973–1,014; Murphy bt Edmonds 1,149–1,073 Losers: £1,000
FINAL:	Russell bt Murphy 1,478–1,058 Loser: £1,500 Winner: £3,000

High break: 268 – M. Russell £300

WORLD CHAMPIONSHIP

The World Championship for the 1989/90 season was scheduled to be held in Australia – too late, unfortunately, for inclusion in this year's edition of the *Benson and Hedges Snooker Year*. Prize money and world rankings, therefore, cannot be finalised.

THE AMATEUR SCENE

IBSF WORLD CHAMPIONSHIP

Ken Doherty, from Dublin's fair city, won the IBSF World Championship at the Ngee Ann Polytechnic in Singapore with an overwhelming 11–2 defeat of Middlesbrough's Jonathan Birch. Doherty was using a cue that cost him just £2. There was no doubt that Doherty, then twenty, was the most outstanding amateur on the circuit and this season he proudly takes his place in the professional ranks. He dominated the final against a strangely out-of-touch Birch who also joins the pro tour this season.

Doherty, the first player from the Republic of Ireland to win the title, started playing as a fourteen-year-old at Jason's Snooker Centre in Dublin. He still uses the cue that he picked up from the rack at the club and for which he had to pay a young member of staff £2 to keep quiet about his 'acquisition'.

Players from the British Isles have dominated this event and it was good to see Franky Chan, from Hong Kong, and Canadian Tom Finstad in the semi-finals. Chan lost 8–2 to Doherty, while Finstad went down 8–1 to Birch.

World champ: Ken Doherty.

BCE ENGLISH AMATEUR CHAMPIONSHIP

Joe Swail became the first Irishman for thirty-eight years to win the BCE English Amateur Championship when he fought off a determined recovery from Glasgow's Alan McManus to score a 13–11 victory and collect the £1,500 first prize. Swail, twenty, from Belfast, looked a comfortable winner as a break of 84 – the highest of the final – gave him a 12–7 lead. But McManus, the Scottish champion, threw caution to the wind and won four frames in a row to leave Swail worried. However,

Irish success: Belfast's Joe Swail (left), the winner, and Alan McManus, the runner-up, after the English Amateur Championship final in Leeds.

nineteen-year-old McManus then missed an easy red and Swail returned to the table to take the frame and the match. An honest Swail said: 'I was glad it didn't go to a last frame decider because I reckon I would have lost. The pressure was getting to me. Now I am very proud for all the people who have helped me back in Northern Ireland.' It was the first final without an Englishman since 1976.

IBSF WORLD JUNIOR CHAMPIONSHIP (AUSTRALIA)

Peter Ebdon, nineteen, staged a stirring recovery to win the IBSF World Junior Championship with an 11–9 victory over fellow Englishman Oliver King at the Clem Jones Stadium in Brisbane, Australia. Ebdon, the number 1 seed and favourite, trailed 7–4 and 9–7 in the final but then, during a five-minute interval, decided on a change of tactics after a 'ticking off' from his manager Joe Terry. 'I slowed my game down and played hit and run snooker,' said Ebdon, from London's Islington, who promptly won four frames in a row. Ebdon is already under contract to Mark McCormack's International Management Group even though he cannot turn professional until next season.

BENSON AND HEDGES CHALLENGE

Euan Henderson made up for his disappointment at missing out on a professional place this season by winning the prestigious Benson and Hedges Challenge in Glasgow. Henderson, a member of Scotland's Home International winning side, was always in control of his final against Falkirk's David Sneddon, the Scottish amateur billiards champion, and came home a deserving 4–1 winner. Breaks of 52 and 51 clinched the last two frames for Henderson who collected a cheque for £2,000. The Challenge is Scotland's richest amateur tournament and produced an entry of more than 3,000 players from 100 clubs.

The champ: Euan Henderson collects his Benson and Hedges Challenge trophy from Bill Faloon of Benson and Hedges.

AMATEUR RESULTS 1989/90

SNOOKER

IBSF World Championship (Singapore)
Ken Doherty (Rep Ire) 11
Jonathan Birch (Eng) 2

BCE English Championship
Joe Swail (Belfast) 13
Alan McManus (Glasgow) 11

IBSF World Junior Championship (Australia)
Peter Ebdon (Eng) 11
Oliver King (Eng) 9

British Isles Under-19
Rod Lawler (Liverpool) 3
Lee Richardson (Oxford) 0

British Isles Under-16
Steve Lee (Wiltshire) 3
Matthew Paffett (Hampshire) 0

BCE Grand Masters
Ted Brown (Suffolk) 4
Roy Andrewartha (Merseyside) 2

UK Pairs
Gary Hill and Robert Foxall (Staffs and
W. Midlands) 3
Gary Baldrey and Lee Richardson
(Northants) 1

Inter-Counties
Cornwall 5
Manchester 4

Inter-Counties Under-19
Essex 5
Yorkshire 4

Pontin's Home Internationals
Winners: Scotland

Daily Mirror/Pontin's Junior Home Internationals
Winners: England

Daily Mirror/Pontin's UK Under-19
Peter Ebdon (London) 4
Richard McDonald (Glasgow) 3

Daily Mirror/Pontin's UK Under-15
Jonathan Saunders (Sheffield) 3
Steve Lee (Wiltshire) 1

Benson and Hedges Challenge
Euan Henderson (Glenrothes) 4
David Sneddon (Falkirk) 1

Rothmans Scottish Championship
Drew Hendry (Rutherglen) 6
Mike Valentine (Glasgow) 2

Associated Leisure National Three-Man Team Championship
Winners: Masters SC (Glasgow)

Hainsworth/TopTable (Billiards and Snooker Federation)
Declan Hughes (NI) 3
Steve Crowley (Sussex) 0

BILLIARDS

English Championship
Martin Goodwill (Lyneham) 2,371
Peter Shelley (Stafford) 1,337   7

British Isles Under-19
Mike Dunn (Cleveland) 363
Sean Golightly (Cleveland) 131

British Isles Under-16
Lee Lagan (Cleveland) 315
Tim Lewis (Wiltshire) 140

Inter-Counties
Yorkshire 1,141
Cambridgeshire 532

Billiards and Snooker Foundation Under-18
David Causier (Cleveland) 388
Conor Morgan (NI) 226

THE INTERNATIONAL BILLIARDS AND SNOOKER FEDERATION

The International Billiards and Snooker Federation (IBSF) now represents more than forty countries worldwide and organises the IBSF World Billiards and Snooker Championships. The IBSF was set up in 1973 and, since 1988, has allowed its members to play for cash prizes since dropping the word 'amateur' from the constitution.

THE BILLIARDS AND SNOOKER CONTROL COUNCIL

The Billiards and Snooker Control Council (B&SCC) is no longer the world governing body, though it still occupies a vital role in the continuing growth of snooker worldwide. The B&SCC controls the copyright of the Rules of Billiards and Snooker, revises the rules, examines and appoints referees and lists all official break and championship records. In addition the B&SCC organises the English and British Isles Championships.

The B&SCC was the governing body of the sports for 100 years until passing over control to the IBSF in 1985.

THE BILLIARDS AND SNOOKER FOUNDATION

The Billiards and Snooker Foundation was established in 1968 to coach young players (male and female) under the age of eighteen in the elementary skills of billiards and snooker. It is jointly financed by the Billiards and Snooker Control Council and the Billiards and Snooker Trade Association.

Courses for coaches are held four times a year at the National Sports Centre in Lilleshall under the guidance of Jack Karnehm, the national coach. There are also places available for coaches from overseas.

In addition the Foundation supplies coaches to operate at Pontin's Holiday Centres, while it runs two tournaments – the Hainsworth TopTable Snooker Championship and the B&SF Under-18 Billiards Championship.

The Coaching Scheme

Prospective coaches must attend a designated course to learn the basic skills of coaching youngsters under the age of eighteen. Qualified coaches are then expected to arrange coaching sessions in their own areas.

Qualifications

A coach should be reasonably proficient at billiards and snooker. He or she should be dedicated to the sport and its advancement, be able to talk freely, clearly and without embarrassment, and be able to communicate easily with others, particularly young people.

Course Syllabus

The aims and objects of the Billiards and Snooker Foundation:

1 Instruction techniques.
2 Basic rules of billiards and snooker.
3 History, characteristics, care and maintenance of equipment.
4 Practical demonstration in instruction.

Examination
A written examination on the basic rules of billiards and snooker. Continuous assessment of candidates takes place during the course.

How to Apply for a Place
To apply for a place on the coaching course write to: Development Officer, Billiards and Snooker Control Council, Coronet House, Queen Street, Leeds LS1 2TN. Every candidate is required to obtain a letter of recommendation from the League or Association with which he or she is connected so that it can be established that he or she conforms to the necessary requirements.

RULES OF THE GAME OF SNOOKER*

Authorised by
THE BILLIARDS AND SNOOKER CONTROL COUNCIL

THE BILLIARDS ASSOCIATION
Established 1885

THE BILLIARDS CONTROL CLUB
Established 1908

AMALGAMATED 1919

Chairman: Stan Brooke
Secretary and Chief Executive: David Ford

SECTION 1. EQUIPMENT

1. Table (Imperial)
1M. Table (Metric)
2. Balls
3. Cue
4. Ancillary

SECTION 2. DEFINITIONS

1. Frame
2. Game
3. Match
4. Balls
5. Striker
6. Stroke
7. In-hand
8. In play
9. On
10. Nominated
11. Pot
12. Break
13. Forced off
14. Foul
15. Snookered
16. Angled
17. Occupied
18. Push-stroke
19. Jump Shot
20. Miss

SECTION 3. THE GAME

1. Description
2. Position of Balls
3. Mode of play
4. Play from in-hand
5. Simultaneous hit
6. Spotting colours
7. Touching balls
8. Edge of pocket
9. Free ball
10. Foul
11. Penalties
12. Movement of ball
13. Stalemate
14. Four handed

SECTION 4. THE PLAYERS

1. Time wasting
2. Unfair conduct
3. Penalty
4. Non-striker
5. Four-handed

SECTION 5. THE OFFICIALS

1. Referee
2. Marker

SECTION 1. EQUIPMENT

1. The Standard Table – Imperial

Dimensions

(a) the playing area within the cushion faces shall measure 11ft 8½ins × 5ft 10ins with a tolerance on both dimensions of ± ½in.

Height

(b) the height of the table from the floor to the top of the cushion rail shall be from 2ft 9½ins to 2ft 10½ins.

Pocket Openings

(c) (i) There shall be pockets at the corners (two at the Spot end known as the top pockets and two at the Baulk end known as the bottom pockets) and at the middle of the longer sides.

(ii) the pocket openings shall conform to the templates authorized by the Billiards and Snooker Control Council.

Baulk-line and Baulk

(d) a straight line drawn 29ins from the face of the bottom cushion and parallel to it is called the Baulk-line and the intervening space termed the Baulk.

The 'D'

(e) the 'D' is a semi-circle described in Baulk with its centre at the middle of the Baulk-line and with a radius of 11½ins.

Spots

(f) four spots marked on the centre longitudinal line of the table.

(i) the Spot: 12¾ins from the point perpendicular below the face of the top cushion.

(ii) the Centre Spot: Midway between the centre pockets and equidistant from the faces of the top and bottom cushions.

(iii) the Pyramid Spot: Midway between the centre spot and the face of the top cushion.

(iv) the Middle of the Baulk-line.

1M. The Standard Table – Metric

Dimensions

(a) the playing area within the cushion faces shall measure 3500 mm × 1750 mm with a tolerance on both dimensions of ± 3 mm.

Height

(b) the height of the table from the floor to the top of the cushion rail shall be from 850 mm to 875 mm.

Pocket Openings

(c) (i) There shall be pockets at the corners (two at the Spot end known as the top pockets and two at the Baulk end known as the bottom pockets) and at the middle of the longer sides.

(ii) the pocket openings shall conform to the templates authorized by the Billiards and Snooker Control Council.

Baulk-line and Baulk

(d) a straight line drawn 700 mm (⅕th the length of the playing area) from the face of the bottom cushion and parallel to it is called the Baulk-line and the intervening space termed the Baulk.

The 'D'

(e) the 'D' is a semi-circle described in Baulk with its centre at the middle of the Baulk-line and with a radius of 292 mm (⅙th the width of the Playing area).

Spots

(f) four spots marked on the centre longitudinal line of the table.

(i) the Spot: 320 mm (⅟₁₁th the length of the playing area) from the point perpendicular below the face of the top cushion.

(ii) the Centre Spot: Midway between the centre pockets and equidistant from the faces of the top and bottom cushions.

(iii) the Pyramid Spot: Midway between the centre spot and the face of the top cushion.

(iv) the Middle of the Baulk-line.

2. Balls

9a) the balls shall have a diameter of 52.5 mm (2⅟₁₆ins) with a tolerance of +00.5 mm −0.08 mm.

(b) they shall be of equal weight within a tolerance of
(i) 3 gms per Snooker set, and
(ii) 0.5 gms per Billiard set.

NOTE: A BALL OR SET OF BALLS MAY BE CHANGED WITH THE CONSENT OF THE PLAYERS OR ON A DECISION OF THE REFEREE.

3. Cue

The cue shall be not less than 910 mm (3ft) in length and shall show no substantial departure from the traditional and generally accepted shape and form.

4. Ancillary

'Rests' may be used to provide a bridge for the cue.

NOTE: IT IS THE PLAYERS RESPONSIBILITY TO BOTH PLACE THE REST ON AND REMOVE IT FROM THE TABLE.

SECTION 2. DEFINITIONS

1. Frame
a frame is completed when
(a) conceded, or
(b) the black is finally potted or fouled.

2. Game
a game is an agreed number of frames.

3. Match
a match is an agreed number of games.

4. Balls
(a) the white ball is the cue-ball.
(b) the 15 reds, and
(c) the 6 colours, are object balls.

5. Striker
The person about to play or in play is the striker and remains so until completion of the stroke or break (Sec. 2 Rules 6 & 12).

6. Stroke
(a) a stroke is made when the striker strikes the cue-ball with the tip of the cue.
(b) for the stroke to be a 'Fair Stroke' the following conditions must be met:
(i) At the moment of striking, all balls must be at rest, and where necesary, colours correctly spotted.
(ii) The cue ball must be struck and not pushed.
(iii) The cue ball must not be struck more than once in the same stroke.
(iv) At the moment of striking, at least one of the strikers feet must be touching the floor.
(v) The striker must not touch any ball other than the cue ball as in section (a) above.
(vi) A ball or balls must not be 'forced off the table'.
(c) a stroke is not completed until all balls have come to rest and the referee has decided the striker has left the table.

7. In-hand
(a) the cue-ball is in-hand when it has entered a pocket or has been forced off the table.
(b) it remains in-hand until played fairly from in-hand or a foul is committed whilst the ball is on the table.

8. Ball in Play
(a) the cue-ball is in play when not in-hand.
(b) object balls are in play when spotted and remain so until pocketed or forced off the table.

NOTE: USING THE CUE TO POSITION THE CUE-BALL
IF THE REFEREE CONSIDERS THE PLAYER IS NOT ATTEMPTING TO PLAY A STROKE, EVEN THOUGH THE TIP OF THE CUE TOUCHES THE CUE-BALL, THE BALL IS NOT IN PLAY.

9. Ball on
Any ball which may be lawfully hit by the first impact of the cue-ball is said to be *on*.

10. Nominated ball
A nominated ball is the object ball which the striker declares, or indicates to the satisfaction of the referee, he undertakes to hit with the first impact of the cue-ball.

NOTE: IF REQUESTED BY THE REFEREE THE STRIKER MUST DECLARE WHICH BALL HE IS ON.

11. Pot
(a) a pot is when an object ball, after contact with another ball, and without any contravention of these rules, enters a pocket.
(b) if a colour, it shall be spotted before the next stroke is made, until finally potted under Sec. 3 Rule 3.
(c) if a stroke is made, with a ball or balls not correctly spotted, and a foul is not awarded, the ball or balls
(i) if on the table will be considered to be correctly spotted.
(ii) if not on the table will be spotted when discovered.

NOTE:
(I) IT IS THE STRIKERS RESPONSIBILITY TO ENSURE THAT ALL BALLS ARE CORRECTLY SPOTTED BEFORE STRIKING.

(II) SUBJECT TO SEC. 3 RULES 8 AND 12, REDS ARE NEVER REPLACED ON THE TABLE DESPITE THE FACT THAT A PLAYER MAY BENEFIT FROM A FOUL.

12. Break
(a) if a ball is potted, the same player plays the next stroke.
(b) a break is a number of pots in succession made in any one turn.

13. Forced off the table.
(a) a ball if forced off the table if it comes to rest other than on the bed of the table or in a pocket.
(b) if a colour it shall be spotted as per Sec. 3 Rule 6 before the next stroke is made.

14. Foul
A foul is any act in contravention of these rules.

15. Snookered
(a) the cue-ball is snookered when a direct stroke in a straight line to any part of every ball *on* is obstructed by a ball or balls not *on*.

NOTE: IF THERE IS ANY ONE BALL THAT IS NOT SO OBSTRUCTED, THE CUE-BALL IS NOT SNOOKERED.

(b) if in-hand, the cue-ball is snookered only if obstructed from all positions on or within the lines of the 'D'.
(c) if the cue ball is obstructed by more than one ball, the one nearest to the cue-ball is the effective snookering ball.

16. Angled
(a) the cue-ball is angled when a direct stroke in a straight line to any part of every ball *on* is obstructed by a corner of the cushion.

NOTE: IF THERE IS ANY ONE BALL THAT IS NOT SO OBSTRUCTED, THE CUE-BALL IS NOT ANGLED.

if angled after a foul,
(b) the referee will state angled ball, and
(c) it may be played from in-hand at the strikers discretion.

17. Occupied
A spot is said to be occupied if a ball cannot be placed on it without it touching another ball.

18. Push Stroke
A push stroke is a foul and is made when the tip of the cue remains in contact with the cue-ball,
(a) when the cue-ball makes contact with the object ball, or
(b) after the cue-ball has commenced its forward motion. PROVIDED that where the cue-ball and an object ball are almost touching, it shall be deemed a fair stroke if the cue-ball hits the finest possible edge of the object ball.

19. Jump Shot
A jump shot is when the cue-ball jumps over any ball except when it first strikes a ball *on* and then jumps over another ball.

NOTE: IF THE CUE-BALL FINISHES ON THE FAR SIDE OF A BALL *ON*, EVEN THOUGH TOUCHING IT IN THE PROCESS, IT IS CONSIDERED TO HAVE JUMPED OVER.

NOTE: AFTER STRIKING THE BALL *ON* FAIRLY IF THE CUE-BALL SHOULD THEN JUMP OVER THAT BALL AFTER HITTING A CUSHION, IT SHALL BE DEEMED TO BE A FAIR STROKE.

20. Miss
A miss is when the referee considers the striker has not endeavoured to hit the ball *on*.

3. THE GAME

1. Description
The game of Snooker is played on an English Billiard Table and may be played by two or more persons, either as sides or independently.

Points are awarded for scoring strokes and forfeits from a opponents fouls.

The winner is the player or side making the highest score or to whom the game is awarded under Sec. 4 Rule 2.

Each player uses the same WHITE cue-ball and there are twenty-one object balls – fifteen reds each valued 1 and six colours: yellow valued 2, green 3, brown 4, blue 5, pink 6 and black 7.

Scoring strokes are made by potting reds and colours alternately until all reds are off the table and then the colours in the ascending order of their value i.e. – yellow through to black.

2. Position of Balls
At the commencement of each frame the object balls are positioned as follows: BLACK on the SPOT; PINK on the PYRAMID SPOT; BLUE on the CENTRE SPOT; BROWN on the MIDDLE of the BAULK-line; GREEN on the LEFT-HAND and YELLOW on the RIGHT-HAND corner of the 'D'.

The reds in the form of a triangle, the ball at the apex standing as near to the pink as possible, without touching it, the base being parallel with and nearest to the top cushion.

NOTE: THE POSITIONS FOR THE OBJECT BALLS ARE COMMONLY REFERRED TO BY THE COLOUR, E.G. BLACK SPOT, PINK SPOT, ETC.

3. Mode of Play
(a) the players shall determine the order of play which (subject to Sec. 3 Rule 10) must remain unaltered throughout the *frame*.

NOTE: THE PLAYER TO STRIKE FIRST AT EACH FRAME SHALL ALTERNATE DURING A GAME.

(b) the first player shall play from *in hand* and the frame starts with the first stroke.
(c) the cue ball
(i) must first hit a ball *on*, and
(ii) must not enter a pocket.
(d) a ball not *on* must not enter a pocket.
(e) (i) for the first stroke of each turn, until all are off the table, red is the ball *on*.
(ii) the value of each red, or ball nominated as red, potted in the same stroke is scored.
(f) if a red is potted, the next ball *on* is a colour, which if potted is scored. The colour is then re-spotted.
(g) (i) until all reds are off the table the break is continued by potting reds and colours alternately.
(ii) the colours then become *on* in the ascending order of their value (Sec. 3 Rule 1) and when potted remain off the table (except as provided for in paragraph (j)).
(h) if the striker fails to score the next player plays from where the cue-ball comes to rest.
(j) when only the Black is left the first score or foul ends the frame, unless the scores are then equal, in which case:

(i) the Black is spotted.

(ii) the players draw lots for choice of playing.

(iii) the next player plays from *in hand* and

(iv) the next score or foul ends the game.

NOTE: AGGREGATE SCORES

IN GAMES OR MATCHES WHERE AGGREGATE SCORES ARE RELEVANT IT IS ONLY WHEN THE SCORES ARE EQUAL AS A RESULT OF THE LAST FRAME THAT THE ABOVE APPLIES.

(k) The striker shall to the best of his ability endeavour to hit the ball *on*. If the referee considers the rule infringed he shall call foul and miss.

NOTE: BALL *ON* IMPOSSIBLE TO BE HIT

IN THIS SITUATION IT HAS TO BE CONSIDERED THAT THE STRIKER *IS* ATTEMPTING TO HIT THE BALL *ON*.

4. To play from in-hand

To play from in-hand the cue-ball must be struck from a position on or within the lines of the 'D'.

NOTE: THE REFEREE WILL ANSWER IF ASKED IF THE BALL IS PROPERLY PLACED.

5. Hitting two balls simultaneously

Two balls, other than two reds or a *free ball* and the ball *on*, must not be hit simultaneously by the cue-ball.

6. Spotting colours

(a) if a colour has to be spotted, and its own spot is *occupied*, it shall be placed on the highest value spot available.

(b) if there is more than one colour, and their own spots are *occupied*, the highest value ball takes precedence.

(c) if all spots are *occupied*, the colour shall be placed as near as possible to its own spot between that spot and the nearest part of the top cushion.

(d) if, in the case of the Black and the Pink, the space between its own spot and the nearest part of the top cushion is *occupied*, the colour shall be placed as near as possible to its own spot on the centre line of the table below that spot.

7. Touching Ball

(a) if the cue-ball is touching another ball which is, or can be, *on*, the referee shall state TOUCHING BALL.

(b) the striker must play away from it or it is a *push stroke*.

(c) no penalty is incurred for thus playing away if:

(i) the ball is not *on*.

(ii) the ball is *on* and the striker *nominates* such ball, or

(iii) the ball is *on* and the striker *nominates*, and first hits, another ball.

NOTE: MOVEMENT OF TOUCHING BALL

IF THE REFEREE CONSIDERS THAT A TOUCHING BALL HAS MOVED THROUGH AN AGENCY OTHER THAN THE PLAYER, IT IS NOT A FOUL.

8. Ball on edge of pocket

(a) if a ball falls into a pocket without being hit by another ball it shall be replaced.

(b) (i) if it would have been hit by any ball involved in a stroke, all balls will be replaced and the stroke replayed.

(ii) if a foul is committed the player incurs the penalty prescribed and all balls will be replaced – subject to Rule 10(c)(ii).

(c) if the ball balances momentarily on the edge and falls in, it must not be replaced.

9. Free ball

(a) after a foul, if the cue-ball is *snookered*, the referee shall state FREE BALL.

(b) if the non-offending player takes the next stroke he may nominate any ball as *on*.

(c) for this stroke, such ball shall (subject to para (e) (i)) be regarded as, and acquire the value of, the ball *on*.

(d) it is a foul, should the cue-ball

(i) fail to first hit, or

(ii) except when only pink and black remain on the table, be *snookered* by, the *free ball*.

(e) if the *free ball* is potted it

(i) is spotted, and

(ii) the value of the ball *on* is scored.

(f) if the ball *on* is potted it is scored.

(g) if both the *free ball* and the ball *on* are potted only the value of the ball *on* is scored (subject to Sec. 3 Rule 3(e)(ii)).

10. Fouls

(a) if a foul is committed:

(i) the referee shall immediately state FOUL and on completion of the stroke announce the penalty.

(ii) unless awarded by the referee or claimed by the non-striker, before the next stroke is made, it is condoned.

(iii) any ball not correctly spotted shall remain where positioned, except that if off the table it shall be correctly spotted.

(iv) all points scored before the foul is awarded or claimed are allowed.

(v) the next stroke is made from where the cue-ball comes to rest.

(b) should more than one foul be committed in the same stroke the highest value penalty shall be incurred.

(c) the player who committed the foul:

(i) incurs the penalty prescribed (which is added to the opponent's score), and

(ii) has to play again if requested by the next player. Once such a request has been made it cannot be withdrawn.

(iii) if a breach of Section 3.3(k) occurs, the offending player has to play again from the original position, if requested by the next player.

11. Penalties

The following are fouls and incur a penalty of four points or the higher one prescribed.

(a) value of the ball *on*:

by striking

(i) when the balls are not at rest (Sec. 2 Rule 6).

(ii) the cue-ball more than once (2–6).

(iii) with both feet off the floor (2–6).

(iv) out of turn (3–3).

(v) improperly from *in-hand* (3–4).

by causing

(vi) the cue-ball to miss all object balls (3–3).

(vii) the cue-ball to enter a pocket (3–3).

(viii) a *snooker* with *free ball* (3–9).

(ix) a *jump shot* (2–19).

(b) value of the ball *on* or ball concerned:

by causing

(i) a ball not *on* to enter a pocket (3–3).

(ii) the cue-ball to first hit a ball not *on* (3–3).

(iii) a *push stroke* (2–18).

(iv) by striking with a ball not correctly spotted (2–11).

(v) by touching a ball with other than the tip of the cue (2–6).

(vi) by forcing a ball off the table (2–13).

(c) value of the ball *on* or higher value of the two balls by causing the cue-ball to hit simultaneously two balls other than two reds or a *free ball* and the ball *on* (3–5).

(d) a penalty of seven points is incurred if:
the striker
(i) after potting a red commits a foul before *nominating* a colour,
(ii) uses a ball off the table for any purpose,
(iii) plays at reds in successive strokes, or
(iv) uses as the cue-ball any ball other than white.

12. Ball moved by other than striker

if a ball, stationary or moving, is disturbed other than by the striker it shall be re-positioned by the referee.

NOTE: THIS COVERS THE CASE IN WHICH ANOTHER AGENCY CAUSES THE STRIKER TO TOUCH A BALL. NO PLAYER SHALL BE RESPONSIBLE FOR ANY DISTURBANCE OF THE BALLS BY THE REFEREE.

13. Stalemate

If the referee considers a position of stalemate is being approached, he should warn the players that if the situation is not altered in a short period of time he will declare the frame null and void. The frame should be re-started with the same order of play.

14. Four-handed snooker

(a) in a four-handed game each side shall open alternate frames, the order of play shall be determined at the commencement of each frame, and must be maintained throughout that frame.
(b) players may change order of play at the beginning of each frame.
(c) if a foul is committed and a request made to play again, the player who committed the foul plays again, and the original order of play is maintained.
(d) when a frame ends in a tie Snooker Rule 3(j) applies. The pair who play the first stroke have the choice of which player plays that stroke. The order of play must then be maintained as in the frame.
(e) Partners may confer during a game but not whilst one is the striker and the striker is at the table or after the first stroke of his break.

SECTION 4.   THE PLAYERS

Time wasting

If the referee considers that a player is taking an abnormal amount of time over a stroke, he should be warned that he is liable to be disqualified.

2. Unfair conduct

For refusing to continue a frame or for conduct which, in the opinion of the referee is wilfully or persistently unfair a player shall lose the game. He is liable to be disqualified from competitions held under the control of The Billiards and Snooker Council and its Affiliated Associations.

3. Penalty

If a game is awarded to a player under this section the offender shall:
(i) lose the game, and
(ii) forfeit all points scored, and the non-offender shall receive the value of the balls still on the table (each red counting eight points).

NOTE: PROVIDED THAT WHERE AGGREGATE POINTS SCORES APPLY, THE OFFENDER SHALL ALSO FORFEIT 147 POINTS FOR EACH UNPLAYED FRAME, TO THE NUMBER REQUIRED TO COMPLETE THE GAME.

4. Non-striker

The non-striker shall, when the striker is playing, avoid standing or moving in the line of sight; he should sit or stand at a fair distance from the table.

5. Absence

In case of his absence from the room he may appoint a substitute to watch his interests, and claim a foul if necessary.

SECTION 5.   THE OFFICIALS

1. The Referee

(a) the referee shall
(i) be the sole judge of fair and unfair play, and responsible for the proper conduct of the game under these Rules.
(ii) intervene if he sees any contravention.
(iii) if a player is colour blind, tell him the colour of a ball if requested.
(iv) clean a ball on a player's request.
(b) he shall not
(i) answer any question not authorized in the Rules.
(ii) give any indication that a player is about to make a foul stroke.
(iii) give any advice or opinion on points affecting play.
(c) if he has failed to notice any incident he may take the evidence of the spectators best placed for observation to assist his decision.

NOTE: THE REFEREE WILL NOT ANSWER A QUESTION REGARDING THE DIFFERENCE IN SCORES.

2. The Marker

The marker shall keep the score on the marking board and assist the referee in carrying out his duties.

NOTE: IF REQUESTED BY THE STRIKER, THE REFEREE OR MARKER MAY MOVE AND HOLD IN POSITION ANY LIGHT SHADE WHICH INTERFERES WITH THE ACTION OF THE STRIKER.

Rules of the
Game of English Billiards*

Authorised by
THE BILLIARDS AND SNOOKER CONTROL COUNCIL

THE BILLIARDS ASSOCIATION
Established 1885

THE BILLIARDS CONTROL CLUB
Established 1908

AMALGAMATED 1919

Chairman: Stan Brooke
Secretary and Chief Executive: David Ford

* Copyright © Billiards and Snooker Control Council

SECTION 1. EQUIPMENT

1. Table (Imperial)
1M. Table (Metric)   3.   Cue
2. Balls   4.   Ancillary

SECTION 2. DEFINITIONS

1.	Game	11.	In-Off
2.	Match	12.	Cannon
3.	Balls	13.	Miss
4.	String	14.	Break
5.	Striker	15.	Forced off
6.	Stroke	16.	Foul
7.	In-hand	17.	Occupied
8.	Ball in play	18.	Push-stroke
9.	Hazard	19.	Jump Shot
10.	Pot		

SECTION 3. THE GAME

1. Description
2. Commencement of Game
3. Order of play
4. Spotting the red ball
5. Details of scoring
6. To play from In-hand
7. Limitations of hazards
8. Limitations of cannons
9. Ball on edge of pocket
10. Ball moved by other than striker
11. Ball touching
12. Miss
13. Fouls

SECTION 4. THE PLAYERS

1.	Time wasting	4.	Non-striker
2.	Unfair conduct	5.	Absence
3.	Penalty		

SECTION 5. THE OFFICIALS

1.	Referee	2.	Marker

SECTION 1. EQUIPMENT

1. The Standard Table – Imperial
Dimensions
(a) the playing area within the cushion faces shall measure 11ft 8½ins × 5ft 10ins with a tolerance on both dimensions of ± ½in.

Height
(b) the height of the table from the floor to the top of the cushion rail shall be from 2ft 9½ins to 2ft 10½ins.

Pocket Openings
(c) (i) There shall be pockets at the corners (two at the Spot end known as the top pockets and two at the Baulk end known as the bottom pockets) and at the middle of the longer sides.
(ii) the pocket openings shall conform to the templates authorized by the Billiards and Snooker Control Council.

Baulk-line and Baulk
(d) a straight line drawn 29ins from the face of the bottom cushion and parallel to it is called the Baulk-line and the intervening space termed the Baulk.

The 'D'
(e) the 'D' is a semi-circle described in Baulk with its centre at the middle of the Baulk-line and with a radius of 11½ins.

Spots
(f) four spots marked on the centre longitudinal line of the table.
(i) the Spot: 12¾ins from the point perpendicular below the face of the top cushion.
(ii) the Centre Spot: Midway between the centre pockets and equidistant from the faces of the top and bottom cushions.
(iii) the Pyramid Spot: Midway between the centre spot and the face of the top cushion.
(iv) the Middle of the Baulk-line.

1M. The Standard Table – Metric
Dimensions
(a) the playing area within the cushion faces shall measure

3500 mm × 1750 mm with a tolerance on both dimensions of ± 3 mm.

Height

(b) the height of the table from the floor to the top of the cushion rail shall be from 850 mm to 875 mm.

Pocket Openings

(c) (i) There shall be pockets at the corners (two at the Spot end known as the top pockets and two at the Baulk end known as the bottom pockets) and at the middle of the longer sides.

(ii) the pocket openings shall conform to the templates authorized by the Billiards and Snooker Control Council.

Baulk-line and Baulk

(d) a straight line drawn 700 mm (⅕th the length of the playing area) from the face of the bottom cushion and parallel to it is called the Baulk-line and the intervening space termed the Baulk.

The 'D'

(e) the 'D' is a semi-circle described in Baulk with its centre at the middle of the Baulk-line and with a radius of 292 mm (⅙th the width of the Playing area).

Spots

(f) four spots marked on the centre longitudinal line of the table.

(i) the Spot: 320 mm (¹⁄₁₁th the length of the playing area) from the point perpendicular below the face of the top cushion.

(ii) the Centre Spot: Midway between the centre pockets and equidistant from the faces of the top and bottom cushions.

(iii) the Pyramid Spot: Midway between the centre spot and the face of the top cushion.

(iv) the Middle of the Baulk-line.

2. Balls

(a) the balls shall have a diameter of 52.5 mm (2¹⁄₁₆ins) with a tolerance of +00.5 mm −0.08 mm.

(b) they shall be of equal weight within a tolerance of

(i) 3 gms per Snooker set, and

(ii) 0.05 gms per Billiard set.

NOTE: A BALL OR SET OF BALLS MAY BE CHANGED WITH THE CONSENT OF THE PLAYERS OR ON A DECISION OF THE REFEREE.

3. Cue

The cue shall be not less than 910 mm (3ft) in length and shall show no substantial departure from the traditional and generally accepted shape and form.

4. Ancillary

'Rests' may be used to provide a bridge for the cue.

NOTE: IT IS THE PLAYERS RESPONSIBILITY TO BOTH PLACE THE REST ON AND REMOVE IT FROM THE TABLE.

SECTION 2. DEFINITIONS

1. Game

A game is completed

(a) at the expiry of a specified period of play, or

(b) when the number of points agreed on is first scored.

2. Match

A match is an agreed number of games.

3. Balls

(a) the cue ball is the ball of the striker.

(b) the other balls are object balls.

4. String

To string is to play together from the Baulk-line to the top cushion with the object of leaving the player's ball as near as possible to the bottom cushion.

5. Striker

The person about to play or in play is the striker and remains so until completion of the stroke or break.

6. Stroke

(a) a stroke is made when the striker strikes the cue-ball with the tip of the cue.

(b) for the stroke to be a 'Fair Stroke' the following conditions must be met:

(i) At the moment of striking, all balls must be at rest, and where necessary, object balls correctly spotted.

(ii) The cue ball must be struck and not pushed.

(iii) The cue ball must not be struck more than once in the same stroke.

(iv) At the moment of striking, at least one of the strikers feet must be touching the floor.

(v) The striker must not touch any ball other than the cue ball as in section (a) above.

(vi) A ball or balls must not be 'forced off the table'.

(c) a stroke is not completed until all balls have come to rest and the referee has decided the striker has left the table.

7. In-hand

(a) A player's ball is in-hand when it is off the table, and

(b) It remains in-hand until played fairly from in-hand or a foul is committed whilst the ball is on the table.

(c) When the non-striker's ball is in-hand it remains so until his turn to play or is spotted as in Sec. 3 Rule 7.

8. Ball in Play

(a) A player's ball is in play when not in-hand.

(b) The red is in play when spotted and remains so until potted or forced off the table.

NOTE: USING THE CUE TO POSITION THE CUE-BALL

IF THE REFEREE CONSIDERS THE PLAYER IS NOT ATTEMPTING TO PLAY A STROKE, EVEN THOUGH THE TIP OF THE CUE TOUCHES THE CUE-BALL, THE BALL IS NOT IN PLAY.

9. Hazard

a hazard is

(a) A pot, or

(b) An in-off.

NOTE: A POT IS OFTEN REFERRED TO AS A WINNING HAZARD AND AN IN-OFF AS A LOSING HAZARD.

10. Pot

A pot is when an object ball, after contact with another ball, and without any contravention of these rules, enters a pocket.

11. In-Off

An in-off is when the cue-ball, after contact with an object ball, and without any contravention of these rules, enters a pocket.

12. Cannon

A cannon is when the cue-ball hits both the object balls, without any contravention of these rules.

13. Miss

A miss is when the cue-ball fails to hit any other ball.

14. Break

A break is a succession of scoring strokes made in any one turn.

15. Forced off the table

A ball is forced off the table if it comes to rest other than on the bed of the table or in a pocket.

16. Foul

A foul is any act in contravention of these rules.

17. Occupied

A spot is said to be occupied if a ball cannot be placed on it without it touching another ball.

18. Push Stroke

A push stroke is a foul and is made when the tip of the cue remains in contact with the cue-ball,

(a) when the cue-ball makes contact with the object ball, or

(b) after the cue-ball has commenced its forward motion. PROVIDED that where the cue-ball and an object ball are almost touching, it shall be deemed a fair stroke if the cue-ball hits the finest possible edge of the object ball.

19. Jump Shot

A jump shot is when the cue-ball jumps over any ball except when it first strikes the object ball and then jumps over another ball.

NOTE: IF THE CUE-BALL FINISHES ON THE FAR SIDE OF THE OBJECT BALL, EVEN THOUGH TOUCHING IT IN THE PROCESS, IT IS CONSIDERED TO HAVE JUMPED OVER.

SECTION 3. THE GAME

1. Description

The game of English Billiards is played by two or more persons, either as sides or independently. Three balls are used, 'plain' white, 'spot' white and red.

It is a game of *pots, in-offs, cannons* and positional play. Points are awarded for scoring strokes and forfeits from an opponents fouls.

The winner is the player, or side, who has scored most points at the expiry of an agreed period, first scores an agreed number of points or to whom the game is awarded under Sec 4 Rule 2.

2. Commencement of Game

(a) The choice of ball and order of play, unless mutually agreed upon, shall be decided by *stringing*, the winner having the option, and shall remain unaltered throughout the game.

(b) At the commencement of the game the red is placed on the spot, the first player plays from *in-hand* and the game starts with the first *stroke*.

3. Order of Play

The players play alternately unless a score is made, in which case the *striker* continues the *break* playing from where his ball rests, or, after an *in-off* or as in Sec, 3 Rule 11, from *in-hand*.

4. Spotting the Red Ball

(a) If the red is *potted* or *forced off* the table it is placed on the spot. If the spot is *occupied* it is placed on the pyramid spot. If that spot is also *occupied* it is placed on the centre spot.

(b) If the red is potted from the spot or pyramid spot twice in succession in one break, not in conjunction with another score, it is placed on the centre spot. If this spot is *occupied* it is placed on the pyramid spot or if both these spots are *occupied* on the spot.
If again potted it shall be placed on the spot.

NOTE: IF DURING A STROKE THE RED COMES TO REST ON THE SPOT, IT IS NOT CONSIDERED TO BE SPOTTED.
IT IS THE STRIKER'S RESPONSIBILITY TO ENSURE THAT ALL BALLS ARE CORRECTLY SPOTTED BEFORE STRIKING.

5. Details of Scoring

Points are awarded as follows:

(a) for a *cannon, pot* white and *in-off* white, two.

(b) for a *pot* and *in-off* red, three.

(c) if more than one *hazard* or a combination of *hazards* and a *cannon* are made in the same *stroke* all are scored.

(d) when an *in-off* is combined with a *cannon* it shall score two or three according to whether the white or red was first hit.

(e) should both be hit simultaneously the *in-off* shall count two.

6. To Play from In-hand

The cue-ball

(a) must be struck from a position on or within the lines of the 'D'.

NOTE: THE REFEREE WILL ANSWER, IF ASKED IF THE BALL IS PROPERLY PLACED.

(b) must hit a ball or cushion out of baulk before hitting a ball in baulk.

(c) may be placed against a cushion in baulk to hit a ball out of baulk.

NOTE: IF THE STRIKER IS IN-HAND THE REFEREE WILL ANSWER, IF ASKED, IF A BALL IS IN OR OUT OF BAULK.

7. Limitation of Hazards

Consecutive *hazards*, not in conjunction with a *cannon*, are limited to fifteen.

If more than one *hazard* is made in the same *stroke* it shall count as one for the purpose of this rule but all points shall be scored.

After ten *hazards*, or on request, the referee shall inform the *striker*.

Should the non-striker's ball be off the table as a result of the non-striker's last stroke, it shall be spotted after the fifteenth *hazard* on the middle spot of the 'D', or if *occupied* on the right hand corner of the 'D'.

NOTE: SHOULD THE REFEREE FAIL TO INFORM THE STRIKER AFTER TEN HAZARDS THE STRIKER IS ENTITLED TO PLAY A FURTHER FIVE HAZARDS AFTER HE IS INFORMED.

8. Limitation of Cannons

Consecutive *cannons*, not in conjunction with a *hazard*, are limited to seventy-five.

After seventy *cannons*, or on request, the referee shall inform the *striker*.

NOTE: SHOULD THE REFEREE FAIL TO INFORM THE STRIKER AFTER SEVENTY CANNONS THE STRIKER IS ENTITLED TO PLAY A FURTHER FIVE CANNONS AFTER HE IS INFORMED.

9. Ball on edge of pocket
(a) if a ball falls into a pocket without being hit by another ball it shall be replaced.
(b) (i) if it would have been hit by any ball involved in a *stroke*, all balls will be replaced and the *stroke* replayed.
(ii) if a foul is committed the player incurs the penalty prescribed.
(c) if the ball balances momentarily on the edge and falls in, it must not be replaced.

10. Ball moved by other than striker
If a ball, stationary or moving, is disturbed other than by the *striker* it shall be repositioned by the referee.

NOTE: THIS COVERS THE CASE IN WHICH ANOTHER AGENCY CAUSES THE STRIKER TO TOUCH A BALL. NO PLAYER SHALL BE RESPONSIBLE FOR ANY DISTURBANCE OF THE BALLS BY THE REFEREE.

11. Balls Touching
When the *striker's* ball remains touching another ball, red shall be placed on the spot, the non-striker's ball, if on the table, shall be placed on the centre spot, and the striker shall play from *in hand*.

12. Miss
(a) For a *miss* the striker incurs a penalty of two points.
(b) a *miss* is a foul except when the striker is *in hand* and there is no ball out of baulk.

13. Fouls
(a) if a foul is committed:
(i) the referee shall immediately state foul.
(ii) unless awarded by the referee or claimed by the non-striker, before the next stroke is made, it is condoned.
(iii) any ball not correctly spotted shall remain where positioned, except that if off the table it shall be correctly spotted.
(iv) all points scored before the foul is awarded or claimed are allowed.
(b) the player committing the foul incurs a penalty of two points, which are added to his opponent's score.
(c) the next player has the option of playing
(i) from where the balls are at rest (the red if off the table having been spotted), or
(ii) from *in-hand*, the red and white being spotted on the spot and centre spot respectively.
(d) the following acts are fouls:
by striking
(i) when the balls are not at rest (Sec. 2 Rule 6).
(ii) the *cue-ball* more than once (2–6).
(iii) with both feet off the floor (2–6).
(iv) out of turn (3–3).
(v) improperly from *in-hand* (3–6).
(vi) with a ball not correctly spotted.

(vii) a ball other than the *cue-ball* (2–6).
by making
(viii) a *jump shot* (2–19).
(ix) a *push stroke* (2–18).
(x) more than fifteen *hazards* (3–7).
(xi) more than seventy-five *cannons* (3–8).
(xii) by touching a ball with other than the tip of the cue (2–6).
(xiii) by forcing a ball off the table (2–6).
(xiv) by using a ball off the table for any purpose.

SECTION 4. THE PLAYERS

1. Time wasting
If the referee considers that a player is taking an abnormal amount of time over a stroke, he should be warned that he is liable to be disqualified.

2. Unfair conduct
For refusing to continue a frame or for conduct which, in the opinion of the referee, is wilfully or persistently unfair a player shall lose the game. He is liable to be disqualified from competitions held under the control of The Billiards and Snooker Council and its Affiliated Associations.

3. Penalty
If a game is awarded to a player under this section the offender shall:
(i) lose the game, and
(ii) if the game was to be decided on a number of agreed points he shall forfeit all points scored and the non-offender shall receive the agreed number of points, or
(iii) if the game be decided at the expiry of a specified period of play and forms part of a team match the whole match shall be forfeited.

4. Non-striker
The non-striker shall, when the striker is playing, avoid standing or moving in the line of sight; he should sit or stand at a fair distance from the table.

5. Absence
In case of his absence from the room he may appoint a substitute to watch his interests, and claim a foul if necessary.

SECTION 5. THE OFFICIALS

1. The Referee
(a) the referee shall
(i) be the sole judge of fair and unfair play, and responsible for the proper conduct of the game under these Rules.
(ii) intervene if he sees any contravention.
(iii) if a player is colour blind, tell him the colour of a ball if requested.
(iv) clean the ball on a player's request.
(b) he shall not
(i) answer any question not authorized in the Rules.
(ii) give any indication that a player is about to make a foul stroke.
(iii) give any advice or opinion on points affecting play.
(c) if he has failed to notice any incident he may take the evidence of the spectators best placed for observation to assist his decision.

NOTE: THE REFEREE WILL NOT ANSWER A QUESTION REGARDING THE DIFFERENCE IN SCORES.

2. The Marker

The marker shall keep the score on the marking board and assist the referee in carrying out his duties.

NOTE: IF REQUESTED BY THE STRIKER, THE REFEREE OR MARKER MAY MOVE AND HOLD IN POSITION ANY LIGHT SHADE WHICH INTERFERES WITH THE ACTION OF THE STRIKER.